Cheap & Easy

A Cookbook for Girls on the Go

SANDRA BARK AND ALEXIS KANFER

Illustrated by VIN GANAPATHY

A FIRESIDE BOOK

Published by Simon & Schuster

New York   London   Toronto   Sydney

FIRESIDE
Rockefeller Center
1230 Avenue of the Americas
New York, NY 10020

For information regarding special discounts for bulk purchases,
please contact Simon & Schuster Special Sales at 1-800-456-6798
or business@simonandschuster.com

Designed by Christine Weathersbee

Manufactured in the United States of America

10 9 8 7 6 5 4 3 2 1

Library of Congress Cataloging-in-Publication Data
Bark, Sandra.
     Cheap & Easy : a cookbook for girls on the go / Sandra Bark & Alexis Kanfer ;
illustrated by Vin Ganapathy.
       p.   cm.
"A Fireside book."
1. Quick and easy cookery. 2. Low budget cookery. I. Title: Cheap and Easy.
II. Kanfer, Alexis. III. Title.
TX833.5 B373   2004
641.5'55—dc22   2004040040

ISBN 0-7432-5054-0

ACKNOWLEDGMENTS

Thanks to everyone who helped us make it happen.

Our agent, Faye Bender at Anderson Grinberg, because it's always more fun when you get to do business with friends.

Vin Ganapathy, the best thing we ever bought online, for the amazing illustrations.

All of the folks at Touchstone Fireside—our insightful editor, Doris Cooper, and her assistants, Sara Schapiro and Katie Myers; our publicists, Marcia Burch and Trina Sisselman; Sybil Pincus, our copyeditor, who really paid attention.

Sarah Masters, recipe testing cruise director, who lent her marketing expertise to our endeavor.

The recipe testers—come over for dinner anytime.

Our families, Bonnie, Dave, Brenda, Mel, Jordan, Ashley, Victoria, David, and Mimi.

Aunt Liz, who let us sit on her porch in Maine and always gives advice.

Molly Boren, the perpetual cheerleader.

Andrew Robertson, tech guy and boy next door.

Diana Chavkin, who brings cookies.

Cheryl Friedman, who offered long-distance support.

All our friends, who let us feed them whenever we asked.

And Princess Pickle and Queen Whimsy, the rulers of our imaginations.

Contents

INTRODUCTION

LITTLE MISS HUBBARD

If you're like us, you enjoy cooking—or want to—but too many recipes seem insurmountable, with ingredients you've never heard of and preparation times that would stress June Cleaver. Sure, we want the gourmet dinner, but there are some major obstacles between us and our three-course meal, like our long day at work, our half-empty refrigerators, and our rumbling stomachs, which *will not wait.*

We all want the good stuff, and we're all tired of spending half our paychecks at the deli counter or on I'll-just-be-really-cheap-tomorrow dinners. We expect gourmet fare, but we don't have the time to baste and caramelize. We're too nutrition-savvy to subsist on fast food, and we need meals that are quick, simple, and inexpensive. Jello Biafra, front man of the iconic '80s punk band the Dead Kennedys, astutely summed it all up when he said, "Give me convenience, or give me death." We want it fast, and we want it now. And there's no way we're moving in with our mothers.

Lucky for us, cooking for ourselves can be cheaper than going out and as easy as heating up a TV dinner. Homemade meals are a lot better for our bodies than the nuclear yellow powder that comes in commercial mac and cheese—and taste better, too. You may still have a futon, but you don't have to live on ramen noodles. Even if you're a lazy Susan.

When you're your own short-order cook, you're in control of how much oil, butter, and sugar make it onto your plate—and you can relax about the ingredients you don't want in your meals, like animal fats for vegetarians and anything you're allergic to or just dislike. No more snooty maître d's: your living room is the perfect setting for a gathering, and you'll be in charge of the menu, the music, and the potential for mischief. So cancel your reservations, crank up the stereo, and get your home fires burning.

Girl, meet spatula.

The recipes in this cookbook are brought to you by two women who created it out of necessity—we wanted good, fast meals on the cheap and easy. We live about ten blocks from each other in downtown Brooklyn. Alexis's studio is near DeKalb Avenue, which bustles with a restaurant row where you can eat in Paris or Cape Town by just crossing the street. Along Fifth Avenue, where Sandra's apartment is, the street is lined with cafés, and the talk and tables spill out onto the sidewalk. When we became friends, we would visit one or another of the local gems, exploring the areas around our homes and enjoying crisp brunch salads, fruity sangria in the evenings, and dizzying desserts on relaxing Sunday afternoons. But we were digging deep craters in our savings accounts, and we needed other options.

Alexis has worked in hot restaurant kitchens and as a caterer to the rich and cranky. She was once a home chef for caloriephobes who refused to eat anything with added fat but kept a closet full of Ding Dongs and Ho Hos hidden away in the basement. Her Key-to-My-Heart Lime Pie makes grown men swoon, and an invitation to brunch at her apartment is like a backstage pass to food heaven. Sandra has been a vegetarian for more than ten years and cooks with a variety of produce, beans, and whole grains. As a cookbook editor, she learned from cooks with whisks in their left hand and pens in their right about translating from the kitchen to the page, how to tell if wine has gone bad, and how to make the perfect omelet.

We had always cooked for ourselves, but then we started cooking for each other. At Alexis's studio, she'd putter in the kitchen while Sandra sat on a barstool cataloging and asking questions. We went to the market together, and Sandra ogled the purple potatoes and the yellow beets while Alexis swooned over the baguettes. Sandra finally bought a hand blender at Alexis's urging, and she can now make olive tapenade (see Olive You, page 71) in less time than it takes to toast a piece of bread. Alexis learned that a bland block of tofu can be prepared to satisfy the finickiest carnivorous taste buds. We stirred and we tasted and we learned what we each did—and did differently—to get fantastic feasts on the table. These banquets and conversations developed into the recipes you are reading now. Together, our cooking styles reflect a fresh, healthy sensibility—perfect for vegetarians and meat eaters alike—that won't make you sacrifice your day or your budget for a fine plateful.

We make these dishes in our homes (our friends always go for seconds), and they were inspired by the selections we order in restaurants, the ingredients on our local grocer's shelves, and meals we've been treated to in the homes of others. Bloody Murray was inspired by an accidental vacancy in our own cupboards. Mark's Breakfast Burrito was created for a cute fireman who just can't say no to a little salsa on a Saturday morning. This cookbook grew out of our own needs, and our own experiences, which we'll share along the way. And you can learn more at www.cheapandeasycookbook.com.

After gathering our recipes, we called for backup. We turned to our friends, who turned to their friends, and more than fifty women (and a few token guys) offered their time and their kitchens to make sure these were recipes for perfection and not for disaster. Cries of "so refreshing!" and "so easy!" flooded our e-mail inboxes. "My boyfriend does all of the cooking in our apartment, but I had no trouble at all with these recipes," said one tester. Another suggested that we "consider putting a warning on the recipe for Love in a Time of Sangria. 'Warning: Too much sangria may lead to love and/or headaches.' " At ranges and counters from the hood to the hills, from Brooklyn to Berkeley, our test drivers let us know what was right—and wrong— with the recipes.

We went back to the kitchen, where we fixed and we fussed, and *Cheap & Easy* evolved into the handy little book you're holding. These recipes are delicious, elegant, and user-friendly. The dishes are fun and healthy, the ingredients are easy to find, and the techniques are simple enough for the most uncoordinated chef. We conquered our kitchens, and you, too, will soon be the master of your culinary domain. Because being prepared means never having to say, "Do you deliver?"

Cheap
&
Easy

BABES IN TOYLAND

Tools of the Trade

Okay, baby. We know you love to shop. There are more than ten thousand Dollar Stores in the country, and all of them are overflowing with the kind of supplies that will help you transform your kitchen into a well-stocked work space without breaking your budget. The same goes for the larger discount stores—Target, Kmart, Wal-Mart—all of which have endless kitchenware sections with gadgets and necessities alike that won't leave you broke.

You may not believe it, but think about this: your kitchen cabinets and bedroom closet have more in common than you realize. Yes, we know you have nothing to wear, but somehow you manage. If you ever decided to toss it all and start from scratch, it would cost heaps of dough to replace those well-worn blue jeans, your favorite cashmere sweater, and even the inexpensive flip-flops you can't do without. But over the years, buying from sample sales here and there and occasionally from higher-priced boutiques when you fall in love and can't walk away empty-handed, you've accrued enough pieces to pull it together every day.

Ditto for the kitchen. As you use your kitchen more, you'll start to realize which implements you'll need to, well, implement. The third time you reach for an extralarge bowl and don't have one, trust us, you'll make your way to the store. That's the way to do it. Stock up on the basics—we've provided a starter list below—and expand from there.

Cookware and Bakeware:

- Mixing bowls: a small, medium, and large bowl, ranging in size from 1 quart to 3 quarts*
- 4 by 9-inch or 5 by 10-inch loaf pan*
- 8 by 8-inch glass baking dish*
- 12-inch skillet or frying pan†
- 2-quart saucepan with lid†
- 4-quart pot with lid†
- Steamer basket
- Cutting board (Plastic or tempered glass is economical and easier to keep clean than wood.)
- 2 baking sheets, preferably nonstick
- 6- and 12-cup muffin tins, preferably nonstick
- Blender (Varieties with more speeds and functions than a racing bike are available at discount stores for under $30.)

Tools:

- Heat-safe spatula
- Wire whisk
- Plastic or glass measuring cup with pouring spout
- Measuring spoons
- Multipurpose grater, for cheese, zest, and ginger
- 8-inch knife (This is often referred to as a "chef's knife," for its usefulness with chopping, mincing, slicing, and dicing. You want a good knife, but you don't need to spend more than you would on a pedicure.)

*Some cookware companies, like Pyrex, sell what they call "starter sets" for around $15 to $20, which include all of the starred items plus handy extras like refrigerater storage lids.

†Same goes for cookware. There are very affordable starter sets that include all of these pots and then some. Those with nonstick interiors that are oven safe are most desirable.

Miscellaneous:

- Aluminum foil
- Clear plastic wrap
- Small and large freezer-safe Ziploc bags
- Food storage containers in assorted sizes, including some single-serving-size ones, preferably microwave safe
- Glass jar with a lid for shaking up dressings, marinades, etc. (Save your next empty jelly jar for such tasks.)
- A few disposable deep-dish rectangular aluminum pans

PANTRY RAID

Shopping List

Late-night raids on your kitchen cabinets can leave you feeling empty. With only a box of stale Saltines and a dusty can of corn on hand, you know you'll be going to bed hungry again. Basic cooking staples will be your salvation. With just a bit of effort, you'll be able to fix yourself a lovely little treat with ease. There's no need to run out and get five varieties of flavored vinegar when one will do. Our pantry list is streamlined so that you'll have what you need and you'll use what you've got.

Pantry:

- All-purpose flour
- Baking powder
- Baking soda
- Brown sugar
- Canned broth—chicken, beef, vegetable
- Canned diced tomatoes
- Canned pitted black olives
- Unsweetened cocoa powder
- Dijon mustard
- Granulated sugar
- Hot sauce
- Inexpensive white wine (Do not buy anything labeled "cooking wine" at the grocery store. The salt content in these products is through the roof.)

- Maple syrup (Aunt Jemima just doesn't cut it. Period. You can find the real stuff in your local grocery store, in specialty stores, or even online. If you're ever on a road trip and pass a farm with a sign that says it has real maple syrup for sale, pull over. A gallon container will last you all year.)
- Olive oil
- Pasta—linguini, penne, or your favorite shape
- Peanut butter
- Salt
- Soy sauce
- Vegetable oil
- White wine vinegar

Spice Rack:

- Black pepper
- Ground cinnamon
- Pure vanilla extract
- Chili powder
- Garlic powder
- Ground ginger
- Curry powder
- Cayenne pepper
- Crushed red pepper flakes

Fridge:

- Eggs
- Milk
- Bread
- Fresh head of garlic
- Unsalted butter
- Fresh lemons and/or limes (or the presqueezed bottled stuff if you prefer)

So there you have it. What used to house a can of beer and your nail polish is now a center of homemaker helpers. Even if you've been misbehaving, you won't have to go to bed without any dinner.

FREEZER FENG SHUI

Making the Most of Your Freezer

To a young lass living on her own, few paths are as well worn as the supermarket aisle that leads to those little frozen dinners. You swing open the heavy door, feel the deep, chill, and remember long ago when these were supposed to be backup, break-glass-in-case-of-emergency, meals. But somehow they've gone from one-night stand to fully committed relationship. Let's face it. Your freezer is a bad neighborhood on the wrong side of town, sis.

Time to summon your cute inner stock boy. Here are the basics:

Baking Soda
Yes, the arm with the hammer. Pop the top and hide that bad boy in a dark corner of the freezer. This will control freezer B.O. for about six months. (You can stick a box in the fridge, too, for extra odor protection.)

Bread
A good loaf of bread from the bakery, presliced and stashed in a freezer-safe plastic bag, is a must. Ten seconds in the microwave and it's like fresh-baked. Pop slices into the toaster for crunchy thick slices of really yummy toast. This bread can also be the basis of your French toast recipe. Remember, good bread is one of the cheapest luxuries you can gift yourself with. And it's great for rounding out a sparse, last-second meal.

Precooked Pasta and Rice
Frozen in freezer-safe plastic zip bags, pasta and rice come back to life quicker than a sleeping beauty. Next time you make pasta or rice, make extra. Making extra is the key, because you are always your own houseguest.

Diced Vegetables
The basic rule of thumb is the less water a vegetable has, the better it freezes. Diced onions, mushrooms, broccoli, peppers, and olives are endlessly fabulous frozen staples to have on hand. Dice 'em and stick 'em in a freezer safe plastic bag or container. Chop now, stir-fry later!

Frozen Herbs
Dried herbs, unfortunately, have a limited shelf life: for maximum freshness and potency, you should use them within a year; some lose their zip in six months. The good news is that you can have farm-fresh herbs year-round. Buy a bunch of your favorite herbs, rinse, and pat dry with a paper towel. Use what you need for now, and freeze the rest for later in an airtight container. The flavor of a frozen herb is almost as vibrant as fresh, and far superior to dried.

Soups and Sauces
Soup can be frozen in small, serving-size containers for easy one- or two-portion defrosting weeks after you've stood over the pot with your glasses fogging. Defrost in the fridge the day before or stick in the microwave for a homemade snack that's ready in minutes. Is there a jar of pasta sauce going to pot in the back of the fridge? Transfer it to a freezer-safe plastic container and save it for another day.

Fruit
Every time you open your refrigerator, you feel a pang of guilt about that pint of strawberries you've meant to use every day since you scored them from that quaint little roadside stand. And now they're furrier than your cat. Don't get blue over abandoned blueberries.

Pop those little guys into the freezer in an airtight container, and save them for pancake batter or smoothies. Peeled bananas, cut into chunks, also freeze exceptionally well.

Bottle of Water

It's always good to have a frozen bottle of water around, especially during the warmer months. Toss it into the trunk with your sandwiches, to keep packed lunches chilly. Carry it in the bottom of your beach bag, and you'll have icy water on the hottest days.

PART ONE

• • • • • • •

GOOD MORNING, SUNSHINE

Breakfasts

Sometimes your morning meal is a leisurely affair—the paper spread out across the table, your fuzzy slippers kicked across the room. Usually, though, you've got half a bagel clamped between your teeth while you fumble with your keys. Different mornings require different strategies, and we've got solutions for all your breakfast situations.

First you'll need to answer some questions.

1. When you eat breakfast, you are usually . . .
    A. Sitting down at the kitchen table
    B. Sitting down in your car with your breakfast on your lap

2. You shower . . .
   A. Before breakfast
   B. While eating breakfast

3. You stand at the counter . . .
   A. To prepare your meals
   B. To eat your meals

4. You skip breakfast . . .
   A. To save room for brunch
   B. Always

5. Your breakfast comes straight out of the . . .
   A. Oven
   B. Box

Scoring: If you're answering mostly A's, you'll want to turn to Easy Like Sunday Morning for great brunch options. This chapter is for those leisurely days when the alarm clock isn't buzzing, when you aren't about to miss your bus, and the knock at the door is not your roommate trying to storm the bathroom with her blow-dryer and beauty tools.

If you're in a real rush, flip to Eat and Run for excellent goodies that you make beforehand and keep in the fridge, on the counter, or even in the freezer. You get to sleep a little later, and you've got a ready-made treat that tucks neatly into your handbag. A healthy breakfast every morning? Just another sign that you're turning into your mother. But we can talk about that later . . .

CHAPTER ONE

EASY LIKE SUNDAY MORNING

Leisure Breakfasts and Brunches

Who said Sunday morning was easy? Your eye makeup is still caked on your lashes (and on your pillow), you can't remember what you did last night, and you're starving. Whether your brunch is tired eyes, sunglasses, and a gaggle of giggling girlies or a newspaper at the corner café, find the Advil and relax. It's easier to whip up a feast than crawl into real clothing and go to a restaurant.

Have the lasses over for Alotta Frittata—they'll bring you flowers and wonder if you finally bucked up for a cooking class. Or invite Mom over for The Independent Pancake. She'll wonder where you learned to do without the pancake mix, and maybe she'll finally give you Grandma's fine china when she sees what a lovely table you set. So invite them to your place, and don't even bother washing your face. Trust us, raccoons are cool.

THE INDEPENDENT PANCAKE

The Pancake Meets the Soufflé

Serves 2 or 3

Prep time: 5 minutes

Cooking time: 12 to 15 minutes

Pancakes are the best, but we hate to be stuck at the stove missing all the good gossip while our guests enjoy themselves at the table. This year's model is our self-sufficient pancake: strong enough for a pan but made for an oven. Instead of twenty or thirty little devils and an oil-splattered apron, you'll have a fluffy, luscious cake that puffs up like a soufflé and must be eaten immediately.

Ingredients

½ cup milk

2 large eggs

¼ cup sugar

½ cup all-purpose flour

3 tablespoons butter

Equipment

Medium mixing bowl

Whisk

12-inch skillet with
　　ovenproof handle

1. Preheat the oven to 425° F.
2. In a medium mixing bowl, whisk the milk, eggs, sugar, and flour, together until just combined. (There will be some lumps.) Set aside.
3. Melt the butter in a 12-inch skillet over medium heat, tilting the pan so the butter is evenly distributed.
4. Pour the batter into the skillet and let it cook on the stove (no stirring) for 1 minute. When the pancake begins to bubble around the edges, gently place the skillet in the oven and bake for 10 to 12 minutes, until the pancake is puffy and golden.
5. Serve with warm maple syrup and seasonal fruit.

Playing the Field

Add these extras to your batter for variation:
- 2 teaspoons cinnamon or 1 tablespoon unsweetened cocoa powder—or both!
- 2 teaspoons vanilla extract
- 1 teaspoon grated lemon zest
- ½ cup chopped pecans
- ½ cup chocolate chips
- ½ cup fresh berries

THE FRENCH TOAST CONNECTION

French Toast with a Crunch

Serves 4

Prep time: 10 minutes

Cooking time: 15 minutes

Any way you slice it, French toast is more than just bread. Especially when you transform this breakfast staple into a special brunch-with-crunch. Serve with yogurt and some fresh berries or warm maple syrup.

Ingredients

3 large eggs

½ cup milk

1 teaspoon cinnamon

2 cups cornflakes, crushed into smaller pieces

8 slices white bread

3 tablespoons butter

Equipment

Foil-lined baking sheet

2 large shallow dishes

Large skillet or griddle

Spatula

1. Preheat the oven to 200° F. Put a foil-lined baking sheet in the oven (to keep prepared slices of French toast warm).
2. In a large shallow dish, beat together the eggs, milk, and cinnamon. Fill another shallow dish with the cornflakes.
3. Soak each slice of bread in the egg mixture for a minute or two, until well saturated, gently flipping bread once. Place the egg-soaked bread slices in the cornflakes, gently pressing down each slice with a spatula so the flakes adhere to the bread. Gently flip the slices over and coat the other side.

4. Melt the butter in a large skillet over medium heat, tilting the pan so the butter is evenly distributed. Add the cornflake-coated slices of bread to the bubbling butter. Cook for 3 to 4 minutes on each side. Transfer the slices to the baking sheet in the oven when thoroughly cooked.

Playing the Field

Add these ingredients to the cornflake mixture for even more wild French toast times:

- ½ cup shredded sweetened coconut
- ½ cup finely chopped nuts: walnuts, pecans, or cashews are all good choices

ALOTTA FRITTATAS

Mini Omelet Cups

Makes 6 individual frittatas
Prep time: 10 minutes
Baking time: 15 to 20 minutes
••••••••••••••••••••••••••••••••

Cousin Sophie hates mushrooms, your roommate is a vegetarian, and your fiancé won't eat onions. What's a brunch-making girl to do? By cooking frittatas in muffin tins, you can customize breakfast for your finicky guests. And the smaller size means a faster baking time!

Ingredients

Butter or oil for greasing pan
2 tablespoons butter, melted
6 large eggs
¾ cup milk
1 tablespoon garlic powder
2 tablespoons all-purpose flour
¼ cup chopped parsley or any
   other aromatic herb
½ cup grated Parmesan cheese,
   optional
Salt and pepper to taste

Equipment

6-cup muffin tin
Large glass measuring
   cup with pouring spout
Whisk

1. Preheat the oven to 425° F.
2. Generously grease a 6-cup muffin tin and set aside.
3. In a large glass measuring cup (or a medium mixing bowl from which you can easily pour the mixture into the greased muffin cups), whisk the butter, eggs, milk, garlic powder, and flour together.
4. Pour the egg mixture into the cups, filling them ¾ full, sprinkle

each cup generously with parsley, and top with some grated Parmesan, if using, and a sprinkling of salt and pepper.

5. Bake for 15 to 20 minutes, until firm and bubbling. Gently coax the frittatas from the muffin tin by running a butter knife around the edges of the cups.

Playing the Field

Add ½ cup of these extras to the egg mixture to kick-start your mini frittatas:

- Bits of crisp bacon or small chunks of ham
- Chopped tomato
- Sliced olives
- Chopped spinach, broccoli, or other greens
- Use more than one type of cheese

COOKING TIP: Using vegetables with a high water content—tomatoes, spinach, broccoli, onions, mushrooms, etc.—tends to create a moister, puffier frittata.

MARK'S BREAKFAST BURRITO

Scrambled Egg or Tofu Breakfast Wrap

Serves 4

Prep time: 10 minutes

Cooking time: 10 minutes

We know two things about our favorite fireman: he loves to surf and he likes only one thing for breakfast. So when sweaty city summers mean the beach is only one Mark-sponsored ride away, we have to do what we can to get him to drop by in the morning. Fully loaded and available in egg or tofu, we've found that making breakfast burritos works better than saying "pretty please."

Ingredients

4 large flour tortillas

2 tablespoons olive oil

1 garlic clove, chopped

1 medium onion, chopped

1 green or red bell pepper,
   chopped

4 large eggs or 1 14-ounce
   package firm or extra-firm
   tofu, drained and cut into
   bite-size cubes

Dash of salt and pepper

1 tablespoon chili powder

2 tablespoons chopped cilantro

Equipment

Aluminum foil

12-inch skillet

Egg Variation

1. Preheat the oven to 200° F. Wrap the tortillas in aluminum foil and put them in the oven to warm.

2. Heat the olive oil in a 12-inch skillet over medium-high heat and sauté the garlic, onion, and bell pepper until the onion is slightly browned at the edges and translucent, about 5 to 6 minutes.

3. Beat the eggs and add them to the skillet. Reduce the heat to medium and scramble the eggs gently without overstirring. (You want fluffy, big pieces of egg, not little tiny curds.) When the eggs lose their "wet look," turn off the heat and sprinkle with the salt, pepper, chili powder, and cilantro.

4. Mix gently and serve wrapped in the warm flour tortillas.

Tofu Variation

1. Preheat the oven to 200° F. Wrap the tortillas in aluminum foil and put them in the oven to warm.

2. Heat the olive oil in a 12-inch skillet over medium-high heat and sauté the garlic, onion, bell pepper, and tofu until the onion is slightly browned at the edges and translucent, about 5 to 6 minutes.

3. When the tofu begins to brown, turn off the heat and sprinkle with the salt, pepper, chili powder, and cilantro.

4. Mix gently and serve wrapped in the warm flour tortillas.

Playing the Field

Try some of these additions:
- A squeeze from a fresh lime wedge
- 1 cup canned black beans, drained and rinsed
- ¾ cup chopped fresh or canned tomato, juices drained
- ½ cup grated Cheddar cheese
- 2 tablespoons canned sliced jalapeño peppers

HOT TO TROT GRITS

Southwestern Spicy Grits

Makes 4 main-dish servings or
6 side-dish servings
Prep time: 5 minutes
Cooking time: 15 minutes

Hot to Trot Grits are a sociable dish—they freeze really well, know how to handle the roughest hangovers, and can sweeten the smile of the surliest cowboy.

Ingredients

1 tablespoon olive oil
1 garlic clove, minced
1 bunch green onions,
   (both white and green parts)
   thinly sliced
1¾ cups canned chicken or
   vegetable broth
1 cup quick-cooking grits
1 cup canned diced tomatoes,
   with juice
1 cup shredded cheese:
   Cheddar or pepper Jack
   work well
Salt and pepper to taste

Equipment

2-quart saucepan

1. Heat the olive oil in a 2-quart saucepan over medium-high heat and sauté the garlic and half the green onions for about 1 minute.
2. Reduce the heat to medium. Add the broth, grits, and tomatoes, stirring frequently. As the mixture thickens, slowly add the cheese

and cook for 10 minutes. (If things get too thick, you can add a dash of milk or water.)

3. Serve piping hot with the remaining green onions sprinkled on top.

Playing the Field

Try these tasty add-ins:
- 1 cup canned corn
- A handful of sliced canned jalapeño peppers
- ½ cup crumbled crisp bacon
- A dollop of cool sour cream on top of the grits

THERE'S NO PLACE LIKE HOME FRIES

Oven-Baked Herbed Potato Wedges

Serves 4

Prep time: 10 minutes

Baking time: 45 minutes to 1 hour

Sometimes a couch potato gets hungry: treat yourself to a side order of diner-fine home fries, served up at home. These go equally well with breakfast or heaped on a plate on a Friday night with lots of ketchup (cat and flick recommended). And even though they taste like they'd be bad for you, they're baked, not fried. But don't worry—you can always rent *Grease.*

Ingredients

2 pounds small red potatoes, scrubbed and cut into large chunks

⅓ cup olive oil

2 garlic cloves, minced

2 teaspoons salt

1 tablespoon pepper

¼ cup fresh, frozen, or dried herbs: parsley, rosemary, basil, thyme, or chives are all good choices

Equipment

large mixing bowl

Foil-lined baking sheet

1. Preheat the oven to 450° F.
2. In a large mixing bowl, combine all the ingredients. (Mix with your clean hands—olive oil has great moisturizing properties!)

3. Spread the potatoes in a foil-lined (easy cleanup!) baking sheet.

4. Bake for 45 minutes to 1 hour, gently turning the potatoes halfway through the baking time. When potatoes are crisp, brown, and aromatic, they are done.

Playing the Field

- Use three large sweet potatoes or yams instead of red potatoes.
- Curry in a hurry: replace the aromatic herbs with 1 tablespoon curry powder and 1 tablespoon brown sugar.

BAKING TIP: For an even crispier potato, run the potatoes under the broiler for just a few minutes before you serve them. A note of caution: the broiler is your oven's full flame and food can burn quickly if not attended. If you're using the broiler, stay nearby and check frequently.

CHIQUITA GRANOLA

Homemade Granola with a Tropical Twist

Makes 6 cups
Prep time: 10 minutes
Baking time: 1 hour

Rediscover your inner hippie. In this homemade granola, bananas act as a binding agent to replace some of the processed sugar and cloying sweetness of store-bought (not to mention the hefty price tag). Deliciously crunchy and tropical, it will keep for a couple of weeks in an airtight container in the fridge.

Ingredients

2 ripe bananas
½ cup brown sugar
¼ cup hot water
1 tablespoon vanilla extract
6 tablesoons melted butter
2 teaspoons cinnamon
4 cups old-fashioned oats
¾ cup diced dried
   pineapple
¾ cup chopped pecans
½ cup shredded unsweetened
   coconut

Equipment

Large mixing bowl
Foil-lined baking sheet

1. Preheat the oven to 275° F.
2. In a large mixing bowl, combine the bananas, brown sugar, hot water, vanilla, butter, and cinnamon. Add the oats, pineapple, pecans, and coconut, and mix well.

3. Spread the mixture onto a foil-lined baking sheet and bake until granola is mostly dry (this will take about 1 hour, depending on your oven). The granola will crisp as it cools.

4. Serve with milk, or over frozen yogurt drizzled with honey, or as a topping for your morning oatmeal.

CHAPTER TWO

EAT AND RUN

Rush Hour Breakfasts

Alarm clock: set for P.M.

Shower water: colder than Christmas morning

Closet: Ghost Town, U.S.A.

Breakfast: With eat-and-run recipes, the baking gets done yesterday so you have a quick breakfast-on-the-go today. Don't forget your vitamin—do we have to do everything for you?

BANANA SPLIT BREAD

Chocolate-Walnut Banana Bread

Makes 1 loaf
Prep time: 10 minutes
Baking time: 45 minutes to 1 hour

If you've ever dreamed of having a banana split for breakfast, why not try our Banana Split Bread? With a rich stripe of chocolate and nuts down the center, banana bread could never be boring. Get last week's bunch of bananas out of the bag and into the batter: the riper the banana, the better the bread.

Ingredients

1½ cups all-purpose flour
1 teaspoon baking soda
1 teaspoon baking powder
¼ teaspoon salt
2 teaspoons cinnamon
1 cup sugar
1 stick unsalted butter,
    softened, plus some for
    greasing pan
2 large ripe bananas, mashed
2 large eggs, beaten
½ cup chopped walnuts
1 cup semisweet chocolate chips

Equipment

Large mixing bowl
Medium mixing bowl
Loaf pan

1. Preheat the oven to 350° F.
2. In a large mixing bowl, combine the flour, baking soda, baking powder, salt, cinnamon, and sugar.

3. In a medium mixing bowl, combine the butter, bananas, and eggs. When these are well mixed, pour over the dry ingredients and combine, taking care not to overmix the batter (it will be a little lumpy).

4. Grease a loaf pan and pour in half the batter. Sprinkle the walnuts and chocolate chips evenly over the batter, and cover with the remaining batter.

5. Bake until a knife inserted into the center of the loaf comes out clean, 45 minutes to 1 hour.

GINGERBREAD GIRL

Peachy Ginger Loaf with Spice Icing

Makes 1 loaf
Prep time: 10 minutes
Baking time: 35 to 45 minutes

The Gingerbread Man might make you chase him, but the Gingerbread Girl is here for you. This peachy ginger loaf is made of sugar and spice and everything nice, a lovely accompaniment to both morning commute and afternoon tea.

Indgredients

3 cups all-purpose flour
2 teaspoons baking soda
1 teaspoon salt
1 tablespoon ginger
2 teaspoons cinnamon
¾ cup brown sugar
1 cup fresh or canned peaches,
   chopped into small pieces
4 tablespoons (½ stick) unsalted
   butter, melted
½ cup maple syrup
2 large eggs
1 cup boiling water

Equipment

Loaf pan or 9 by 9-inch
   baking pan
Large mixing bowl
Medium mixing bowl
Small mixing bowl

Spice Icing

¾ cup confectioners' sugar
   (powdered sugar)
3 tablespoons milk
1 teaspoon cinnamon
1 teaspoon ginger

1. Preheat the oven to 375° F.
2. Grease a loaf pan or a 9 by 9-inch baking pan and set aside.
3. In a large mixing bowl, combine the flour, baking soda, salt, ginger, cinnamon, and brown sugar.
4. In a medium mixing bowl, combine the peaches, butter, maple syrup, and eggs.
5. Slowly start adding the wet ingredients to the flour mixture. Last, add the boiling water. Remember not to overmix the batter, which can cause the bread to toughen.
6. When all the ingredients have been combined, pour the batter into the loaf or baking pan and bake until a knife inserted into the center comes out clean, 35 to 45 minutes, depending on your oven. Because of the fruit, this is a moist cake, so use your eyes: if the cake is brown around the edges and pulling away from the pan, and the knife comes out clean, your gingerbread is done.
7. In a small mixing bowl, combine all the Spice Icing ingredients. Add more milk or confectioners' sugar as needed to produce an icing with a consistency you can drizzle over the gingerbread.

THE CORN STAR

Cornbread or Corn Muffins

Makes 6 muffins or 1 pan
Prep time: 5 minutes
Baking time: 20 to 30 minutes
• •

Hey, muffin—want to be the star of an adult breakfast? Cornbread is a wholesome treat that will give you the energy to be naughty. Come on, Debbie. Do breakfast.

Ingredients

1⅓ cups yellow cornmeal
⅔ cup all-purpose flour
¼ cup sugar
1 tablespoon baking powder
1 tablespoon baking powder
1 teaspoon salt
1 cup milk
4 tablespoons (½ stick) butter
    or margarine, melted

Equipment

6-cup muffin tin, or 8 by 8-
    inch or 9 by 9-inch baking
    pan
Large mixing bowl
Medium mixing bowl
Whisk

1. Preheat the oven to 425° F.
2. Grease a 6-cup muffin tin or an 8 by 8-inch or 9 by 9-inch baking pan and set aside.
3. In a large mixing bowl, combine the cornmeal, flour, sugar, baking powder, and salt.
4. In a medium mixing bowl, combine the milk and butter and add to the cornmeal mixture, whisking gently until just combined.
5. If you're playing the field, now is the time to add your extra ingredients. You don't want to overmix—just combine until everything is well integrated.

6. Spoon the batter into the muffin cups or pour into the baking pan and bake for 20 to 30 minutes, until golden brown on top and a knife inserted into the center comes out clean.

Playing the Field

Playing the field is second nature to The Corn Star. Here are some lusty combos:

- ½ cup chopped green onion and 2 tablespoons toasted sesame seeds
- ¼ cup crisp bacon bits and ½ cup grated Cheddar cheese
- 1 tablespoon chili powder and ½ cup chopped cilantro

COOKING TIP: Nuts and seeds can be toasted on your stovetop over medium heat in a small skillet until lightly browned.

PART TWO

• • • • • • •

LADIES WHO LUNCH

Lunches

Do you suffer from limp lettuce?

Do you run for the blue plate special to avoid the blue
   bologna in your fridge?

Is your restaurant habit eating into your new shoe habit?

Does the hot dog vendor outside your office wave at you
   when you walk by?

Does the Chinese takeout joint lady know your order by heart?

Yes to any of these questions means that this section is one you should
read carefully. After all, if you love your lunch, you're more likely to
make time to eat it. With selections for simply satisfying lunches at
home, and strategies for lunching on the go, our midday menu is
chick-tested and dude-approved. And don't forget the lunch potential
of innovative leftovers. Eat well yesterday, reheat happily today.

   Here's to the ladies who lunch.

CHAPTER THREE

WELL DRESSED

Dressings

People pay attention to the way you dress: a salad dressing can take simple greens from daytime to evening with just a splash. Whether you're in the mood for light or creamy, mild or tangy, you won't have to visit any hidden valleys—the perfect vinaigrette is as close as your kitchen cupboard.

Welcome to our Dressing Room.

ORANGE GODDESS

Carrot-Ginger Dressing

Makes 1 cup

Prep time: 5 minutes

The delectable tangy-sweet dressing that your hunk of iceberg swims in at the sushi bar is siiiiinfully easy to re-create at home. Make extra. This is the chocolate chip cookie dough of salad dressings—you'll be drinking from the blender before you get it near your greens!

Ingredients

3 medium carrots, peeled and cut into chunks

2-inch piece of fresh ginger, peeled

1 tablespoon soy sauce

¼ cup white wine vinegar

¼ cup orange juice

2 tablespoons peanut oil

Equipment

Blender

In a blender, combine all the ingredients except the oil. Pulse blender until the mixture is mostly smooth, then add the oil and puree for 15 seconds. (Blending oil for too long emulsifies it, giving it a mayonnaise flavor you don't want in this dressing.)

From the Field

- Iceberg lettuce
- Green pepper
- Cucumber
- Chopped peanuts

MEANWHILE, BACK AT THE RANCH

Creamy Tofu Ranch Dressing

Makes 1 cup
Prep time: 5 minutes
••••••••••••••••••••••

Versatile tofu stands in for dairy in this creamy, distinct dressing. Low in fat, high in protein—so good there's no need to wait for the cows to come home to enjoy it.

Ingredients

¾ cup silken or soft tofu
3 tablespoons olive oil
¼ cup white wine vinegar
1 garlic clove, finely minced
1 teaspoon salt
1 teaspoon pepper
¼ cup chopped herb of
    your choice: parsley, cilantro,
    or dill works well

Equipment

Small mixing bowl
Whisk

In a small mixing bowl, combine all the ingredients except the herb. Whisk together, then add herb last (overmixing herbs will turn your dressing green).

From the Field

- Cucumber
- Tomatoes
- Red onion
- Feta cheese

COLONEL MUSTARD
Tangy Mustard Dressing

Makes ¾ cup
Prep time: 5 minutes

Whodunnit? Colonel Mustard, in the kitchen with a whisk, that's who. There's no mystery to preparing this savory dressing, since it's made from ingredients you've already got on hand. So get a clue.

Ingredients

¼ cup Dijon mustard
¼ cup olive oil
2 tablespoons white wine
    vinegar
Salt and pepper to taste

Equipment

Small mixing bowl and
    whisk, or glass jar with lid

Whisk all the ingredients together in a small mixing bowl. Or put everything in a glass jar with a lid and shake. Voilà!

From the Field

- Mixed greens
- Fresh peas
- Mushrooms
- Cubed ham

MEMOIRS OF A GRAPEFRUIT

Zesty Citrus Dressing

Makes 1 cup
Prep time: 5 minutes

This light and crisp dressing is the essence of dressing well. Elegant, pure flavors shine through. Serve over crisp mixed greens.

Ingredients

½ cup fresh grapefruit juice
   (approximately the juice of
   1 grapefruit)
1 teaspoon grated grapefruit
   zest
¼ cup olive oil
1 tablesoon honey
Salt and pepper to taste

Equipment

Small mixing bowl and
   whisk, or glass jar
   with lid

Whisk all the ingredients together in a small mixing bowl. Or put everything in a glass jar with a lid and shake, shake, shake. You're done!

From the Field

- Arugula
- Toasted hazelnuts
- Dried cranberries
- Sliced turkey (Buy it ready-made at the deli.)

VERMONT, ITALY, VINAIGRETTE

Maple Balsamic Dressing

Makes 1 cup
Prep time: 1 minute
•••••••••••••••••••••

If Vermont were in Italy, we're sure someone would have thought of this simple dressing. A great marriage of sweet and tangy, there are few things finer than mixing tender spinach leaves with strawberries, pecans, and this lovely dressing.

Ingredients

¼ cup pure maple syrup
⅔ cup balsamic vinegar

Equipment

Small mixing bowl and
    whisk, or glass jar
    with lid

Whisk all the ingredients together in a small mixing bowl. Or put everything in a glass jar with a lid and shake.

Playing the Field

Simmering your balsamic vinegar over a low flame for a few minutes before mixing your dressing makes it extra kicky. We learned that trick from our friend Ben, who used his dressing skills to convince his dates to, well, undress. Co-opt his technique and see if it works on guys, too. Or try mixing your straight or reduced balsamic with some olive oil and adding some raspberry jam or Dijon mustard.

From the Field

- Spinach
- Strawberries, mandarin orange segments, or apple slices
- Pecans
- Red onion

GET YOUR CROUTON ON

Crunchy Garlic Croutons

Makes 2 cups
Prep time: 5 minutes
Baking time: 15 to 20 minutes

A terrific way to use your stale bread, add crunch to your salad, and keep vampires away.

Ingredients

3 tablespoons olive oil
1 large garlic clove,
    finely chopped
1 tablespoon dried herbs:
    oregano, parsley, etc.,
    optional
Salt and pepper to taste
2 cups bite-size cubes made
    from day-old French bread

Equipment

Large mixing bowl
Whisk
Foil-lined baking sheet

1. Preheat the oven to 350° F.
2. In a large mixing bowl, whisk together the olive oil, garlic, and herbs, if using, adding salt and pepper to taste. Toss the bread cubes in the mixture until evenly coated.
3. Spread the croutons on a foil-lined baking sheet (no cleanup!) and bake for 15 to 20 minutes, or until they are very dry and lightly golden.

CHAPTER FOUR

SOUPED UP

Soups

Who doesn't love soup? In our book, if you can eat it with a spoon, it's already our favorite. We've got hot soups for cold days, cold soups for hot days, chunky soups for when you want a whole meal in a bowl, and light soups for when you're feeling chunky.

Our recipes aren't much harder than hitting Start on the microwave. And without all the sodium and MSG of their totally processed canned cousins, your homemade soup will taste nice and you'll still be able to fit into those pants tomorrow.

FRED AND GINGER PUMPKIN SOUP

Pumpkin-Ginger Soup

Serves 4

Prep time: 5 minutes

Cooking time: 15 to 20 minutes

Finally, a pumpkin soup you don't have to dance backward in high heels for. This cancan is the easiest lineup around: canned broth means less cooking time, and canned pumpkin means no seeds on the floor to get in the way of your two-step.

Ingredients

One 15-ounce can chicken
   or vegetable broth
One 15-ounce can pumpkin
   (about 2 cups)
1 cup cream, milk,
   or silken tofu
1 tablespoon ground or
   grated fresh ginger
Salt and pepper to taste
Chopped chives, optional

Equipment

4-quart pot

In a 4-quart pot, combine all the ingredients, except the chives, add salt and pepper to taste, and bring just to a boil. Reduce the heat to heat medium-low and simmer uncovered for 15 minutes. If you are using milk instead of cream or tofu, you might want to add a little bit of extra pumpkin for thickness. Serve warm, garnished with chives, if desired.

Playing the Field

Try adding these alternate flavors to your pumpkin soup:

- 2 tablespoons curry powder for an exotic
  island flavor
- 1 teaspoon freshly grated nutmeg and
  1 teaspoon cinnamon for a soothing and
  spicy taste of autumn

CHICK'S PEA STEW

Rustic Chickpea Stew

Serves 4

Prep time: 5 minutes

Cooking time: 25 minutes

Even if your pad doesn't have a fireplace, you'll be getting cozy on a winter's eve with our hearty homemade stew. Ladies, start your blenders.

Ingredients

3 tablespoons olive oil
1 small onion, chopped
2 garlic cloves, minced
One 15-ounce can chicken
   or vegetable broth
One 15-ounce can chickpeas
   (garbanzo beans)
One 15-ounce can diced
   tomatoes, with juice
Salt and pepper to taste

Equipment

4-quart pot
Blender

1. Heat the olive oil in a 4-quart pot over high heat. Add the onion and garlic, reduce the heat to medium, and sauté, stirring occasionally, until the edges of the onion are browned, about 5 minutes.

2. Add the broth, chickpeas, and tomatoes and simmer slowly for 20 minutes, uncovered, stirring occasionally.

3. Carefully transfer a few cups (but not all) of the mixture to a blender and pulse ingredients for 5 to 10 seconds (pulse is a standard quick chopping speed on most blenders). Check the consistency with a spoon. The idea is to partially puree some of the soup,

which adds a thick and creamy consistency without the added fat of butter or cream.

4. Add the pureed soup to the pot and combine with the remaining coarse bits of beans and vegetables. Add salt and pepper to taste. Serve hot.

Playing the Field

- Add a cup of red or white wine to the broth while you are simmering to add depth and flavor to your soup.
- Add a few small red potatoes cut into wedges for a stew that is even more rustic and hearty.
- If you don't have a blender, or you just don't like to wash it, don't stress. This stew is fantastic even when eaten with a fork.

DON'T FRENCH KISS ME ONION SOUP

Modern French Onion Soup

Serves 4
Prep time: 15 minutes
Cooking time: 30 minutes

You may not get much action after eating a bowl of this oniony broth, but your mouth will be so satisfied you won't even care. Before making this soup, remember that big girls do cry: try putting the onions in the freezer for 20 minutes prior to cutting to avoid a sob story.

Ingredients

1 tablespoon butter
2 tablespoons olive oil
2 large onions,
   very thinly sliced
1 tablespoon sugar
1 cup red wine
Two 15-ounce cans beef,
   chicken, or vegetable
   broth
3 tablespoons chopped
   thyme, chives, or parsley
Salt and pepper to taste
4 slices bread (you should
   have some in your freezer,
   ladies!)
1 cup mild white cheese, shredded:
   mozzerella, provolone, or Swiss—
   any of these will work

Equipment

4-quart pot with a lid
Foil-lined baking sheet
Glass or coffee mug
   (to use as cookie cutter)

1. Preheat the oven to 450° F.

2. Combine the butter and olive oil in a 4-quart pot over medium heat. (We're using a mixture here because butter imparts a delicious flavor but burns more easily than olive oil. Since we'll be cooking the onions for a while, and olive oil can withstand a higher heat, we'll combine the two.) Add the onion slices (they will fill the pan but will wilt down quickly as you cook them) and cook, stirring occasionally to coat the onion with butter and olive oil. When the onion starts to brown, add the sugar. Continue cooking until the onion is glossy, light brown, and wilted into long strands, about 15 minutes.

4. Add the wine, broth, and 2 tablespoons of the herbs, and add salt and pepper to taste. Simmer, covered, over low heat for 10 to 15 minutes to allow the flavors to come together.

5. Lay the bread on the baking sheet and cut rounds using the mouth of a large glass or coffee mug. (Discard the excess bread.) Sprinkle generously with the cheese. Toast gently in the oven for 5 to 7 minutes, or until golden and bubbling.

6. Garnish each bowl of soup with a toasted cheese round and a sprinkling of the remaining tablespoon of herbs.

Voilà! C'est magnifique!

IT'S-A-RENTAL RED LENTIL SOUP

Red Lentil Soup

Serves 4
Prep time: 5 minutes
Cooking time: 30 minutes

Red lentils are tiny, orange, and cute as a button. Littler lentils cook faster, and dried beans are about the best cheap protein you can buy. So when rent is due and you can't get out of hosting the book club your best friend made you join, serve this soup with some cheap red wine and a really crusty loaf of bread, and you'll feed a table full of people happily on what you'd normally spend to blow out your hair.

Lentil soup gets better the next day. Leftovers are a special gift you can leave for yourself or anyone who might pass through your home, so even if you aren't cooking for a group, don't be tempted to make less than a full pot.

Ingredients

2 tablespoons olive oil
1 medium onion, chopped
2 garlic cloves, chopped
2 carrots, finely chopped
Generous handful of minced
   fresh, dried, or frozen herbs:
   parsley, cilantro, basil, or
   oregano are all good choices
1½ cups dried red lentils, rinsed
1 cup wine, red or white
½ cup soy sauce
Salt and pepper to taste

Equipment

4-quart pot with a lid

Heat the olive oil in a 4-quart pot over medium heat and sauté the onion for a few minutes until shiny and translucent. Add the garlic, carrots, and herbs. Add the lentils to the pot and add enough water to cover. Add the wine and the soy sauce, and add salt and pepper to taste. Simmer, covered, for 20 minutes.

Playing the Field

- Try adding different vegetables: red peppers, white potatoes, yams, zucchini, celery, or squash.
- A tablespoon of ground or treated fresh ginger and 2 tablespoons of toasted sesame oil will add a delicious Asian flavor to the soup.

GIRLSPACHO

Spicy Chilled Vegetable Soup

Serves 4

Prep time: 15 minutes

Hey, girlie. Cool things down in the hotter months with our version of this classic cold soup.

Ingredients

3 large, ripe tomatoes,
   peeled
Large handful of chopped
   cilantro
1 garlic clove, minced
One 15-ounce can
   vegetable broth
2 tablespoons olive oil
½ cup bread crumbs
1 small red onion,
   finely diced
1 large cucumber, peeled,
   seeds scooped out with
   a spoon, and cut into
   small cubes
Salt and pepper to taste

Equipment

Blender

1. Cut the tomatoes into quarters and place in the blender container along with the cilantro, garlic, and vegetable broth. Pulse the blender for 5 to 10 seconds to combine the ingredients.

2. Add the olive oil, then add the bread crumbs, and give the blender one more pulse.

3. Put the onion and cuke in a decorative bowl or pitcher (that's how it's served in Pedro Almodóvar's *Women On the Verge of a Nervous Breakdown*) and pour the tomato mixture on top. Stir to combine, and add salt and pepper to taste.

4. Refrigerate and serve chilled.

Playing the Field

Golden Girlspacho: For a more modern and mature soup, you don't have to be a swinging senior; try using yellow tomatoes instead of red, for 14-karat fun.

THE BIG CHILI

Hearty One-Pot Chili

Serves 4
Prep time: 15 minutes
Cooking time: 45 minutes

Just because it's below freezing out, there's no need for the cold shoulder. Icy days call for warming measures—grab an extra pair of socks and heat things up with this simmering stew.

Ingredients

2 tablespoons olive oil
1 large onion,
    coarsely chopped
2 garlic cloves, minced
1 pound skinless, boneless
    chicken breasts, cut into
    bite-size chunks, or 1 pound
    ground turkey or beef
One 12-ounce can beer or
    1½ cups red or white wine
One 15-ounce can diced
    tomatoes, with juice
2 tablespoons chili powder
2 tablespoons hot sauce,
    optional

Equipment

4-quart pot

1. Heat the olive oil in a 4-quart pot over medium-high heat. Add the onion and garlic and sauté until the edges of the onion are slightly browned.

2. Add the meat, reducing the heat if necessary and stirring occasionally to keep things from sticking. When the meat is just cooked through, 5 to 6 minutes, add the beer or wine, tomatoes, chili powder, and hot sauce, if using.

3. Bring the mixture to a boil, reduce the heat, and simmer, uncovered, until any liquid is reduced and your chili is nice and thick—about 45 minutes.

Playing the Field

It isn't whether you win or lose, it's how you play the field. To complete your chili and make it colorful and delicious, include your choice of:

- 1 cup diced green, red, or yellow bell pepper (Sauté with onion and garlic.)
- 1 cup diced celery (Sauté with onion and garlic.)
- 1 cup chopped carrots (Sauté with onion and garlic.)
- 1 cup frozen corn kernels (Add after you brown the meat.)
- ½ cup canned green chilis, drained and chopped (Add after you brown the meat.)
- One 15-ounce can white beans, garbanzo beans (chickpeas), or kidney beans, drained and rinsed (Add after you brown the meat.)

CHAPTER FIVE

LUNCH BOX

Beyond Soups and Salads

What's in your lunch box? If flimsy white-bread sandwiches just don't cut it, turn the pages for some lunchtime treats that pack up easily for work or picnics and make great couch companions if you're enjoying a leisurely lunch at home. With our quick quiches, updated sandwiches, and perfect mac and cheese, you'll be able to stay on top of your afternoon and keep the hunger pangs at bay. If you're in the mood, invite someone over to share—it's just as easy to cook for two, and then you can guilt someone else into doing the dishes.

QUICHE AND MAKE UP

Savory Quiche

Serves 4
Prep time: 10 minutes
Baking time: 35 to 40 minutes

So you borrowed your best friend's ex, and she ruined the suede boots you lent her. We're not saying she didn't do it on purpose, but please, relax. You both need to cool down and realize there's no need to bicker. In the future, though, you don't need to share *everything*. And when you're ready to kiss and make up, you can try one of our humble pies.

Ingredients

2 tablespoons olive oil
1 small onion, chopped
1 cup frozen chopped
   spinach, defrosted in
   the microwave
4 large eggs
1 cup grated Swiss cheese
½ cup milk or cream
½ teaspoon salt
1 teaspoon pepper
½ teaspoon freshly grated
   nutmeg, optional
1 9-inch refrigerated, or frozen
   and slightly defrosted, ready-to-
   bake pie crust (not the dessert
   graham cracker kind, but the
   savory dough kind)

Equipment

12-inch skillet
Medium mixing bowl
Baking sheet

1. Preheat the oven to 375° F.

2. Heat the olive oil in a 12-inch skillet over medium-high heat. Add the onion and sauté until the edges are slightly browned, about 5 to 6 minutes. Add the spinach and stir together. Turn off the heat.

3. In a medium mixing bowl, beat the eggs, cheese, milk, salt, pepper, and nutmeg, if using, together.

4. Add the spinach-onion mixture to the egg mixture and stir. When the filling is well combined, pour it into the pie crust. Fill just to the inside rim of the crust, as the filling will expand and need room to grow on top.

5. Put the quiche on the baking sheet and bake for 35 to 40 minutes, or until the egg is set and a knife inserted in the center comes out clean.

Playing the Field

Expand your quiche vocabulary: use Cheddar or Parmesan cheese instead of Swiss; try broccoli instead of spinach; add olives or roasted red pepper.

Lunch Box

Pack a slice for work in a container, along with a container of Chick's Pea Stew (page 50) or a salad with Meanwhile, Back at the Ranch (page 41) dressing.

MAC AND JILL

Grown-up Macaroni and Cheese

Serves 6

Prep time: 15 minutes

Baking time: 30 to 40 minutes

It's all fun and games until someone falls down and breaks that crown. Take a time-out and have a nice old-fashioned lunch dish: the star of school lunches and SoHo restaurants, mac and cheese is our favorite childhood staple, a treat that's more classic than kitschy.

Ingredients

8 ounces elbow macaroni
3 tablespoons butter
3 tablespoons all-purpose flour
2 cups milk
2½ cups shredded Cheddar cheese
1 teaspoon salt
1 teaspoon pepper
1 teaspoon garlic powder
½ cup toasted bread crumbs

Equipment

4-quart pot
2-quart saucepan
9 by 9-inch baking dish

1. Preheat the oven to 350° F.
2. Cook the macaroni in a 4-quart pot according to package directions, and keep an eye on it as you prepare the cheese sauce.
3. Melt butter in a 2-quart saucepan over medium-high heat. Add the flour and stir briefly. Add the milk to the butter and flour mixture and bring just to a boil, then reduce the heat to medium.

Add 2 cups of the Cheddar cheese (reserve ½ cup to sprinkle on top) and stir until the sauce becomes thick and creamy. Add the salt, pepper, and garlic powder.

4. When the macaroni is cooked, drain, then pour into a buttered 9 by 9-inch baking dish. Pour the hot cheese sauce over the macaroni, and sprinkle the bread crumbs and remaining ½ cup cheese over the mixture.

5. Bake for 30 to 40 minutes, until the top is golden and bubbling.

Lunch Box

Mac and cheese to go: pack for lunch in a container, along with a container of green salad with Colonel Mustard (page 42).

ROMEO AND JELLY

Updated Classic Sandwiches

Makes 1 sandwich
Prep time: 2 minutes
....

Love doesn't need to end with broken hearts. Check your lo-cal gourmet grocery for nut butters and sophisticated jellies—we've reinvented this dynamic duo to help you reconnect with your after-school sweetheart.

Some suggestions:
- Almond butter, peanut butter, cashew butter
- Fig jelly, pear jelly, mango preserves, or any flavor that appeals to you
- Add a layer of fruit: sliced apples or pears, dates, banana slices (try it drizzled with honey!).
- Try dried cranberries or golden raisins.
- Toast. Shmear. Slice. Layer. Build. Cut on the diagonal.

Lunch Box

Take the romance on the road, or to the park. Wrap two sand-wiches in aluminum foil and pack in a paper bag with a baggie of cut carrots and a bag of potato chips. And if your beau isn't there yet when you arrive, for God's sake, wait a few minutes before you do anything rash.

CURRY UP!

Curried Chicken Salad

Serves 2
Prep time: 5 minutes
Cooking time: 20 minutes

Wait not, want not. You're hungry and don't want to stand on line at the deli. Served on a green salad, or in a sandwich, this delectable dish is the cure for the common lunch.

Ingredients

2 large skinless, boneless chicken breasts (about 1 pound)
½ cup light or regular mayonnaise
1 teaspoon honey
2 teaspoons curry powder
1 teaspoon ginger
¼ teaspoon salt
¼ teaspoon pepper
¼ cup thinly sliced green onion (both white and green parts)

Equipment

2-quart pot with a lid
Large mixing bowl

1. Place the chicken breasts in a 2-quart pot with just enough hot water to cover them.
2. Simmer gently, covered, for 15 to 20 minutes, never letting the liquid boil. This technique, known as poaching, produces juicy chicken. Slice one of the breasts in half; you'll know it's fully cooked when it's no longer pink in the center. If the chicken is done, set it aside to cool.

3. In a large mixing bowl, combine the mayo, honey, curry powder, ginger, salt, and pepper. Mix well.

4. When the chicken is cool enough to handle, cut it into bite-size cubes and toss with the mayo mixture. Add a little more mayonnaise if you want, until the salad is the consistency you like. Last, add the green onion. Refrigerate and serve chilled.

Playing the Field

Take your curry to the next level with a sprinkling of:
- ½ cup cashews or pecans
- ½ cup golden raisins
- ½ cup red seedless grapes
- ½ cup coarsely chopped celery

Lunch Box

Make a sandwich on your favorite bread or in a pita. Wrap Curry Up! in foil and bring along in a paper bag with an apple and some cut-up celery. And stop dawdling!

RELISH THE THOUGHT

Sweet Onion Relish

Makes 1 cup
Prep time: 15 minutes
Cooking time: 20 minutes
••••••••••••••••••••••••••••

So, you've been dreaming about lunch since 8 A.M. This sweet onion relish is sinfully good—and makes a heavenly cheese sandwich. Try it on hamburgers and steak, or smeared on grilled chicken breasts, too. The relish will keep for up to a week in your fridge in an airtight container.

Ingredients

2 tablespoons olive oil
2 cups diced red onion
1 teaspoon salt
¼ cup white wine vinegar
1 tablespoon brown sugar

Equipment

2-quart saucepan

Heat the olive oil in a 2-quart saucepan over high heat. Sauté the onion and salt for 2 minutes, then reduce the heat to medium. Stir frequently to keep the onion from sticking and burning. When the onion starts to soften and turn brown around the edges, add the vinegar and brown sugar. Continue to cook until the mixture is soft, brown, and aromatic, about 30 minutes.

Playing the Field

To spice up your relish, try the following additions:
- 1 tablespoon ground or grated fresh ginger
- 1 teaspoon cayenne pepper

Lunch Box

Spread some relish on two slices of French bread and add a nice thick slice of white cheddar. Wrap the sandwich in foil and bring along with a container of It's-a-Rental Red Lentil Soup (page 54) and enjoy the idea of your lunch as much as your actual lunch.

OLIVE YOU

Olive Tapenade

Makes a scant cup
Prep time: 5 minutes
....

An easy way to let them know you care. Serve on a crusty baguette with mozzarella and fresh tomatoes for a loving sandwich, or as an appealing appetizer with a loaf of bread (set out alongside a dish of balsamic vinegar and olive oil topped with oregano and parsley).

Ingredients

1 cup pitted Kalamata olives
¼ cup pine nuts
¼ cup chopped fresh
   or dried basil
2 tablespoons olive oil

Equipment

Medium mixing bowl
Blender (optional)

Finely chop all the ingredients and toss together. (For a smoother spread, use a hand blender or upright blender and pulse all the ingredients until smooth.)

Lunch Box

Wrap your mozzarella sandwich and pack along with Fred and Ginger Pumpkin Soup (page 48) in the winter or Girlspacho (page 56) in the summer. Or lose the soup and go for a salad with Vermont, Italy, Vinaigrette (page 44).

WRAPSODY
Asian Chicken or Tofu Wrap

Makes 2 wraps
Prep time: 10 minutes
Cooking time: 10 minutes

Peanut sauce is a joyful accompaniment to this Asian-inspired wrap. So are the compliments your lunch companion will undoubtedly throw your way.

Ingredients

Filling
1 tablespoon olive oil
1 tablespoon soy sauce
Dash of cayenne pepper
2 large skinless, boneless
   chicken breasts (about
   1 pound), cut into strips,
   or 1 14-ounce package
   extra-firm tofu, drained
   and cut into strips
2 8-inch flour tortillas
1 cup shredded lettuce
½ cup thinly sliced carrots,
   optional
2 tablespoons thinly sliced
   green onion (both white
   and green parts)

Equipment
Medium mixing bowl
Medium skillet
Small mixing bowl

Peanut Sauce

¼ cup peanut butter

2 tablespoons hot water

1 tablespoon soy sauce

½ teaspoon garlic powder

1 teaspoon ground or grated fresh ginger

1. In a medium mixing bowl, combine the olive oil, soy sauce, and cayenne pepper, then marinate the chicken or tofu in the mixture for a few minutes.

2. Heat the skillet, then add the chicken or tofu and marinade and sauté over medium-high heat until cooked through.

3. Top the tortillas with the lettuce, carrots, if using, green onion, and chicken or tofu.

4. To make the peanut sauce, whisk all the ingredients together in a small mixing bowl.

5. Roll your wraps, drizzle with peanut sauce, and serve.

Lunch Box

Wrap in foil, grab some fresh fruit, and you're good to go.

PART THREE

● ● ● ● ● ● ●

GOOD LIBATIONS

Beverages

Get out the margarita glasses—it's time to bid adieu to cotton mouth and say adios to water-from-the-tap. You can kiss the container good-bye, say *sayonara* to the soda fountain, and send a note of regret to the barman. With icy drinks for sultry eves and steaming mugs for frigid mornings, whether you're a Boozie Betty or a Betty Ford, we've got some liquid lovin' for you.

CHAPTER SIX

LIKE A VIRGIN

Nonalcoholic Drinks

Forget Shirley Temple—we're talking Lolita. We know you can toss them back when the moment calls for it, but perhaps this time you'd like something more subdued to sip while the gentlemen pound their beers. Whatever your pleasure, you can warm up or cool down with one of our innocent tantalizers. You don't even have to put down your lollipop.

SODA JERK

Egg Cream Soda

Serves 1
··········

Time to play ice cream shoppe—without dealing with the surly soda boy. The egg cream (which has never been made with eggs) hails from 1920s New York City; see our Playing the Field version to celebrate the end of Prohibition, which thankfully ended in 1933.

Ingredients

2 tablespoons chocolate or vanilla syrup
⅓ cup cold milk
½ cup seltzer

Spoon syrup in a tall, cool glass. Stir in milk, then add seltzer. Stir and serve.

Playing the Field

For a Drunk Jerk, add ⅓ cup Baileys or other similar Irish cream liqueur and use 1 tablespoon of the flavored syrup.

MANGO LASSIE

Mango Yogurt Shake

Makes 2 servings
....

This is our version of *lassi,* a traditional Indian yogurt drink. Delicious, low-fat, and thoroughly refreshing: fruit-at-the-bottom, begone! For this shake, choose mangoes that are bursting with ripeness and feel soft when you poke 'em.

Ingredients   Equipment

1 cup low-fat plain yogurt   Blender
2 mangoes
1 tablespoon honey

Combine all the ingredients in the blender until smooth.

Playing the Field

Try these substitutions and additions
- Vanilla yogurt instead of plain yogurt
- ½ cup orange juice
- 1 teaspoon ground cardamom (available in the spice aisle of most supermarkets or at Indian grocery stores)
- 1 teaspoon cinnamon

COCOA CHANEL

Homemade Hot Chocolate Mix

Makes 20 servings
••••••••••••••••••••

Say au revoir to those store-bought ready-to-wear packets and whip up some of our *haut chocolat.* This fast, homemade hot chocolate mix may be cheap and easy, but it tastes like it was made especially for you. (Great for camping trips, too.)

Ingredients

2½ cups dry powdered
   whole milk
1 cup sugar
¾ cup unsweetened cocoa powder
¾ cup powdered nondairy creamer
½ teaspoon salt

Equipment

Plastic storage container
   with tight-fitting lid

1. Combine all the ingredients in a plastic storage container. Tightly secure the lid, and shake well to mix.
2. To serve, mix 2 to 3 tablespoons of mix with 6 ounces of boiling water.

CHAI ME UP, CHAI ME DOWN

Indian Spiced Tea

Makes 2 servings

Everywhere we go, chai makes an appearance. You've seen it on grocery store shelves and at crunchy cafés. Now you can make your own at home. Delicious hot or iced, but we have to warn you: once you pick it up, it's hard to put down.

Ingredients

2 tablespoons loose
   black tea
1-inch piece of fresh ginger,
   peeled and cut into several
   smaller pieces
1 teaspoon vanilla extract
10 black peppercorns
5 cloves
2 cinnamon sticks
1 cup whole milk
¼ cup honey

Equipment

2-quart saucepan
Strainer
Small mixing bowl

1. Bring 2 cups of water, the tea, ginger, vanilla, peppercorns, cloves, and cinnamon sticks to a boil in a 2-quart saucepan. Turn down the heat and simmer. Let steep for 10 minutes, then strain into a small mixing bowl. Discard solids.
2. Pour the strained liquid into the saucepan and add the milk and honey. For hot chai, stir well and serve immediately.

3. For iced chai, let the mixture cool down and serve over ice cubes. This keeps very well in the fridge.

Playing the Field

Add these to the original spice mixture:
- 5 cardamom pods
- 3 pieces star anise

ALONG CAME A CIDER

Mulled Apple Cider

Makes 4 servings
....

Perfect for an autumn get-together, you should make this cider about an hour or so before the crowd descends. The flavors will meld and the gorgeous aroma of citrus and spices will make your friends think that they've stumbled into a heavenly orchard instead of your cobwebbed quarters.

Ingredients

4 cups apple cider (available year-round in most supermarkets)
2 oranges, sliced (do not peel)
10 to 15 cloves
4 or 5 cinnamon sticks
¼ cup brown sugar

Equipment

2-quart pot with lid

Pour the cider into a 2-quart pot. Stud the orange slices with the cloves and add to the cider along with the cinnamon sticks and brown sugar. Bring just to a boil and reduce the heat. Cover and simmer gently for 15 to 20 minutes. Pour into 4 mugs (leave in the orange slices and the cinnamon sticks) throw another log on the fire, and kick back!

Playing the Field

Fill mugs ¾ full and top off with a generous splash of light, dark, or spiced rum.

CHAPTER SEVEN

LUSH HOUR

Alcoholic Drinks

Once you hit twenty-one, there was no stopping you. (We won't mention the ID your cousin gave you when you were sixteen.) But years of ordering at the bar has been a drain on the wallet, and you're ready to bring the party home.

These delightful drinks will have you dancing like a showgirl in just a few sips—but don't drink too fast, or you might end up under the table instead of on it. Included in this chapter are concoctions for summer afternoons, snowy evenings, anytime-of-the-year brunches, and dance-till-you-die-or-the-sun-comes-up throw downs.

Plus, we've thoughtfully included some noshes that can be enjoyed with only one hand, leaving the other free to hold your glass. With these delightful nibbles, you can wet your whistle without whining about it the next day. So, take a load off, fanny, and mix up one of our obliging libations.

IF LIFE HANDS YOU VODKA

Spiked Watermelon Lemonade

Makes 4 servings
·····················

You should know by now that you've got to make your own luck—and while you're at it, make some for your lucky friends, too. Summer watermelon or berries are lovely with vodka and some lemonade. A porch and a swing are a nice garnish, but a few mint leaves will suffice.

Ingredients

4 cups lemonade, fresh
   squeezed, from a carton,
   or from concentrate
2 cups cubed watermelon
1 cup vodka or flavored
   vodka: raspberry, citrus,
   vanilla
A few sprigs of mint

Equipment

Pitcher
Blender (optional)
Strainer

1. Pour the lemonade into a pitcher.
2. Mash the watermelon (or swirl in a blender, if you've got one), strain. Add to the lemonade and stir.
3. Add the vodka.
4. Pour into tall glasses over ice.
5. Garnish each glass with a sprig of mint.

Playing the Field

Use 1 cup of your favorite berries instead of watermelon.

BLENDERELLA

Blended Fruit and Spirits

Makes 2 servings
....

It's nearly midnight and you still haven't started drinking? Take off the glass slippers, princess. What do you need, a personal invitation? A blender plus your favorite spirits and fresh berries will impress your fairy godmother and any other pre-party guests. And so quick, you won't even be late to the ball.

Ingredients

3 ounces tequila, vodka,
   or light rum
1 cup orange juice
2 tablespoons fresh lime juice
½ cup sliced strawberries
2 teaspoons sugar

Equipment

Blender

In a blender, combine all the ingredients with 6 or 8 ice cubes. Blend until smooth.

Playing the Field

Don't be a one-fruit wonder! Try these other combinations:
- Strawberries and blueberries
- Pineapple and raspberries
- Mango and banana

LOVE IN A TIME OF SANGRIA

Wine and Fruit Punch

Makes 6 to 8 drinks
••••••••••••••••••••••

Sangria is the perfect date drink. Wine mingles with luscious slices of ripe fruit and other flavors in a pitcher. Served in dark, exotic cafés from Buenos Aires to Barcelona, we invite you to stir up some trouble of your own. Be creative—like love, sangria comes in many different forms.

Ingredients	Equipment
1 bottle of inexpensive red wine	Pitcher
1 cup juice: apple, orange, or pineapple all work well	
2 cups club soda	
1 cup brandy, optional	
2 cups assorted fruit, cut into bite-size cubes and wedges: apples, oranges, lemons, limes, pears, pineapple, melon, or pitted cherries are all good selections	

Mix wine, fruit juice, club soda, brandy, if using, and fruit together in a pitcher. Serve well chilled.

Playing the Field

Try white wine instead of red; try rum, Cointreau, Grand Marnier, or Midori instead of brandy.

BLOODY MURRAY

Our Version of the Bloody Mary

Makes 1 drink
....

Catch a buzz and rediscover your Jewish heritage: we made Bloody Marys one fine day—without the Worcestershire, since it's made with anchovies and Sandra is a vegetarian—and then realized we were out of celery. We did have a jar of kosher pickles, and so our Bloody Murray tradition was born. The dill spear makes a good crunchy stirrer. And a Bloody Murray goes just as well with Alotta Frittatas as a nice toasted bagel.

Ingredients

2 ounces vodka
¾ cup tomato juice
Dash of Worcestershire sauce
   (or soy sauce for vegetarians)
Dash of hot sauce
Squeeze from a fresh lemon or
   lime wedge
Pinch of black pepper
Kosher or dill pickle spear tall
   enough to stick out of the glass

Mix all the ingredients except the pickle and pour over ice. Garnish with a pickle spear.

TEQUILA MOCKINGBIRD

Tomorrow's Headache

Makes 1 drink

Ingredients

1 bottle of tequila
1 shot glass

Drink neat.
Repeat as needed.
You will be mocked mercilessly the next day.
Guaranteed.

HOT AND BOTHERED

Laced Dessert Coffees

Makes 1 drink
••••••••••••••••

If you like your coffee like you like your men—strong, rich, and alcoholic—look no further for the perfect beverage. You may not have a working fireplace, but if you're looking for a hot night, you can get warm and snuggly with these no-brainer after-dinner coffee recipes. Just don't expect to get any sleep. And don't say we didn't warn you. (Also appealing in the afternoon with a blanket and Scrabble.)

Per ¾ cup of strong brewed coffee:
  If you like hazelnuts, try adding
      ¼ cup Frangelico.
  If you like chocolate, try adding ¼ cup
      Godiva chocolate liqueur.
  If you like Irish cream, try adding ¼ cup
      Baileys.

Add milk if you like. And a little whipped cream on top never hurt anyone, either (see You're Whipped!, page 126).

NICE TODDY

Hot Rum and Spices

Makes 1 drink
••••••••••••••••

Nothing heats you up like a nice hot toddy. Let it simmer on the stove while you slip into woolly socks. Set the steaming mug down while you tuck the blanket around yourself. Drink slowly while you enjoy the pleasures of a good book, some mindless television programming, or the attentions of a favorite companion.

Ingredients

Slices of lemon or orange
(do not peel)
Sugar to taste
Spiced rum

Equipment

Medium saucepan

In a medium saucepan combine water, lemon, sugar, and let simmer. Pour into mug and top off with rum.

Playing the Field

For a Nicer Toddy, add grated fresh ginger, a few whole cloves, and a cinnamon stick to the saucepan.

PART FOUR

· · · · · ·

SUPPER CLUB

Dinners

We know all your dinnertime excuses—you're tired and hungry (and you can't wait), you cooked yesterday, there's nothing in the house, the pizza around the corner is so tempting . . .

We get it, we get it. You barely have enough time to unwind in the evening, let alone spend an hour in the kitchen after a day of filing, faxing, phoning, and freaking out. Or a day of shopping, getting your nails done, and hitting the park for a nice jog.

But you still have to eat.

Our myriad dinner choices take the pain out of dinner preparations with simple, ingredients-on-hand recipes that fit every eater, budget, and time crunch. Kick your ramen noodle habit and still catch the last few minutes of *Will and Grace.* No matter who's at your house, including you, good food is always the best company.

CHAPTER EIGHT

MAIN SQUEEZE

Entrées

Check out our intriguing entrées. With a range of choices from stir-fries to pasta to mix'n'match meatloaves, and suggestions for getting dinner on the table when you've been standing at the fax machine all day, our roster of main attractions is designed to keep your attention from wandering at the end of the day.

MOJITO PORK

Sweet and Spicy Pork Stir-fry

Serves 4
Prep time: 15 minutes
Cooking time: 20 minutes

We like mojitos so much we wondered why we couldn't have them for dinner every day. Now you can, using the classic drink ingredients to add a fresh spin to your plain old meat and veggies. Fresh mint, lime, honey, and rum lend bright flavors to this versatile dish.

Ingredients

Equipment

Marinade

¼ cup soy sauce
1 teaspoon grated lime zest
Juice of 2 limes
1 tablespoon hot sauce
2 tablespoons honey
2 garlic cloves, minced
¼ cup chopped cilantro or mint

1 pound ½-inch-thick boneless
   pork loin chops, cut crosswise
   into ⅓-inch-wide strips

Olive oil
1 large onion, chopped
1 large bell pepper (any color),
   thinly sliced
¼ cup light rum

Medium mixing bowl
Large skillet

Sprigs of cilantro or mint
Lime wedges

1. In a medium mixing bowl, combine the soy sauce, zest, lime juice, hot sauce, honey, garlic, and cilantro. Mix well and add the pork strips. Marinate the pork for at least 20 minutes, or overnight if you have the time.

2. Heat the olive oil in a large skillet and sauté the onion and pepper over medium-high heat until lightly browned, about 3 to 5 minutes. Add the pork strips, reserving the marinade for use later. Stir-fry until the pork is cooked through, another 3 to 4 minutes. Remove the cooked pork, onion, and pepper to a plate or bowl.

3. Add the reserved marinade to the skillet. Turn the heat up to high, and when the mixture starts to bubble, stir in the rum. The sauce will begin to thicken. When it reduces to the consistency of a glaze, return the pork, onion, and pepper to the pan to coat. Stir a few seconds just to combine all the ingredients.

4. Serve over rice, garnished with sprigs of fresh cilantro and a lime wedge.

Playing the Field

COULD IT BE ... SEITAN?

Vegetarian Version of Mojito Pork

Even the church lady couldn't find anything sinful about stir-fried seitan—except the taste. Made from wheat gluten, these faux meaty bits are surprisingly satisfying when done right. Substitute one pound of seitan for the pork in this recipe.

GIRL MEETS SOY

Simple Tofu Steak

Serves 4
Prep time: 10 minutes
Baking time: 15 minutes

Bad soys give tofu a lousy reputation. Luckily, a good recipe is all you need to meet the soy of your dreams. This one is almost too easy—and great served hot with Rice Capades (page 115) and Green Party (page 116), or sliced from the fridge into sandwiches the next day.

Ingredients

2 14-ounce packages
    extra-firm tofu
3 tablespoons olive oil
½ cup soy sauce

Equipment

Plates for pressing tofu
Baking sheet
Aluminum foil

1. Preheat the oven to 400° F.
2. Press the tofu blocks between two plates until the water drains, about 5 to 10 minutes, then slice the pressed tofu in half lengthwise.
3. Line a baking sheet with aluminum foil and fold up the edges to keep in the juices so there's no baked-in greasy pan to wash. Put the tofu steaks on the baking sheet and rub them liberally with the olive oil and soy sauce.
4. Bake for 15 minutes.

Playing the Field

Try drizzling your tofu steaks with any of these tasty additions:
- Hot sauce
- Asian sesame oil
- Barbecue sauce
- Sesame seeds (can be toasted, if you like, in a small skillet on your stovetop)

SHADY LADY
PASTA PUTTANESCA

Pasta with Spicy Olive Tomato Sauce

Serves 2

Prep time: 10 minutes

Cooking time: 15 minutes

Pasta *puttanesca* is rumored to have been the cheap and easy dinner of choice for Italian streetwalkers, which is how it got its name. This recipe for a fragrant and hearty pasta can easily be doubled—serve it with lots of crusty bread and a nice bottle of wine to your hardworking friends.

Ingredients

8 ounces penne pasta

3 tablespoons olive oil

3 large garlic cloves,
   coarsely chopped

½ cup pitted black olives,
   chopped

½ cup red or white wine

2 tablespoons capers, drained,
   optional

Generous handful of chopped
   flat-leaf parsley

1 teaspoon crushed red pepper
   flakes

1 15-ounce can diced tomatoes,
   with juice

Salt and pepper to taste

Equipment

4-quart pot

2-quart saucepan

1. Cook the pasta in a 4-quart pot according to package directions until al dente (slightly chewy but not undercooked).

2. Heat the olive oil in a 2-quart saucepan over high heat. Add the garlic and reduce the heat to medium. Sauté lightly, adding the olives, wine, capers, if using, parsley, and red pepper flakes.

3. Simmer, uncovered, for 2 to 3 minutes and then add the tomatoes, letting the whole mixture cook down over medium-high heat to the consistency of a chunky sauce.

4. Adjust seasoning to taste before serving. Pour over the pasta.

MIX 'N' MATCH MEATLOAF

One Recipe, Many Meatloaves

Serves 4
Prep time: 10 minutes
Baking time: 1 hour
....

Our basic recipe is a masterpiece all its own, but you can still be a meatloaf Matisse and play the field here. We won't tell anybody if you want to pass this off as your grandma's recipe . . .

Ingredients

1½ pounds ground beef
   or turkey
¾ cup bread or cracker
   crumbs
1 large egg, beaten
1¼ teaspoons salt
1 teaspoon pepper
¾ cup ketchup
2 tablespoons brown sugar
1 small onion, minced
2 teaspoons garlic powder

Equipment

Large mixing bowl
Your well-washed hands
Loaf pan or foil-lined
   baking sheet

1. Preheat the oven to 350° F.
2. In a large mixing bowl, combine all the ingredients. Wash up well and really get in there with your hands—the best mixing tool around—then transfer the mixture to a loaf pan. You can also free-form a loaf with your hands and bake it on a foil-lined baking sheet.
3. Bake for 1 hour. Let the meatloaf stand for 5 minutes before slicing.

Playing the Field

Add these extras to the basic recipe for a meatloaf makeover:
- *BBQ Meatloaf:* Substitute ¾ cup barbecue
  sauce for the ketchup and add 2 tablespoons
  of your favorite mustard.
- *Teriyaki Meatloaf:* Add ½ cup chopped water
  chestnuts, ½ cup chopped green onions (both
  white and green parts), and ¼ cup soy sauce.
- *Italian Meatloaf:* Substitute 1 cup of store-bought
  marinara sauce for the ketchup, and add ½ cup
  grated parmesean cheese and 1 tablespoon chopped
  fresh or dried basil.

LAZY GIRL'S LASAGNA

A Fuss-Free Version of Your Favorite

Serves 4
Prep time: 20 minutes
Baking time: 1 hour

Old-fashioned lasagna recipes called for the noodles to be boiled first and then painstakingly laid out on the counter, making this delicious dish seem messy and time-consuming. With the discovery of precooked noodles, even slackers can make grandma-fine trays of perfect lasagna without chipping their manicures. This lasagna is so cheap and easy, we should put a leash on it and make it our mascot! And it freezes extremely well, so don't be afraid to wrap and freeze individual servings for homemade TV dinners.

Ingredients

1 32-ounce jar of your
   favorite spaghetti sauce
1 cup red wine or water
3 cups ricotta cheese or
   small-curd cottage cheese
2 garlic cloves, minced
2 tablespoons mixed dried
   herbs: try basil, oregano,
   and parsley
1 large egg, beaten
1 teaspoon salt
1 teaspoon pepper
1 teaspoon freshly grated
   nutmeg, optional

Equipment

Small mixing bowl
Medium mixing bowl
Disposable deep-dish
   rectangular aluminum
   pan
Aluminum foil

1 pound dried precooked
   lasagna noodles
2 cups shredded mozzarella
   cheese

1. Preheat the oven to 375° F.

2. In a small mixing bowl, combine the spaghetti sauce with the wine.

3. In a medium mixing bowl, combine the ricotta, garlic, herbs, egg, salt, pepper, and nutmeg, if using.

4. In a deep-dish rectangular pan long enough to fit your lasagna noodles, start by spreading a ½-inch-thick layer of the sauce on the bottom of the pan. Follow with a layer of slightly overlapping noodles. Next, add a layer of the ricotta mixture, a layer of sauce, another layer of noodles, another of ricotta, and so forth, alternating layers of sauce, ricotta, and noodles until you are about an inch and a half from the top of the pan, at which point you will want to top off the lasagna with the mozzarella cheese.

5. Cover the pan with aluminum foil and bake for 45 minutes. Take the foil off and let the lasagna bake, uncovered, for 15 to 20 minutes or until the cheese is slightly browned and bubbling. Remove the lasagna from the oven and allow it to rest for 10 to 15 minutes before serving, to ensure nice clean slices.

WINGS OF DESIRE

Honey-Ginger Chicken Wings

Serves 2

Prep time: 10 minutes

Baking time: 30 to 40 minutes

They want you to want them—sweet spicy wings get a kick from ginger and a crunch from chopped peanuts that you won't be able to resist.

Ingredients

⅔ cup soy sauce

½ cup orange juice

¼ cup honey

1 tablespoon ground or
   minced fresh ginger

2 garlic cloves, minced

3 pounds chicken wings
   (15 to 20 wings)

½ cup coarsely crushed
   salted peanuts

1 bunch green onions, cut
   into thin diagonal slices

Equipment

Large mixing bowl

Foil-lined baking sheet

1. Preheat the oven to 400° F.

2. In a large mixing bowl, combine the soy sauce, orange juice, honey, ginger, and garlic. Mix well and add the chicken wings. Marinate the wings for at least 1 hour, or overnight if you have the time. Make sure to turn the wings at least once, as the marinade will not cover the wings completely.

3. Remove the wings from the marinade, place them on a lightly oiled, foil-lined baking sheet and put them in the oven. These wings get juicy, so you might need to pour off a little bit of the liquid that will accumulate while they're baking.

4. When the wings are golden brown, after 30 to 40 minutes, remove them from the oven, sprinkle with the peanuts and green onions, and serve.

ON THE BARBIE

Oven-Baked Apple Barbecue Chicken

Serves 4
Prep time: 10 minutes
Baking time: 35 to 45 minutes

You don't have a real outdoor grill or a plastic boyfriend named Ken—but you can still transform boring chicken breasts into fantastic oven-baked barbecue.

Ingredients

One 15-ounce can diced
   tomatoes, with juice
¼ cup soy sauce
1 tablespoon chili powder
¼ cup white wine vinegar
¼ cup maple syrup or honey
2 garlic cloves, minced
4 skinless, boneless chicken
   breasts, about 2 pounds total
1 large apple, cored, peeled,
   and cut into large chunks
1 large onion, cut into
   large wedges

Equipment

Large mixing bowl
Foil-lined baking dish

1. Preheat the oven to 375° F.
2. In a large mixing bowl, combine the tomatoes, soy sauce, chili powder, vinegar, maple syrup, and garlic. This will be your home-made barbecue sauce.
3. Place the chicken breasts in a foil-lined baking dish and scatter the cut-up apple and onion around them. Pour the barbecue sauce

over the chicken, apple, and onion, and bake for 35 to 45 minutes, until the chicken breasts are tender and cooked through.

Playing the Field

Try canned or fresh pineapple instead of the apple for another fruity twist.

NO DISH FISH

Foil-Packet Fillets

Serves 2
Prep time: 10 minutes
Baking time: 10 to 15 minutes

Look, Ma—no dish! Foil-packet cooking means no cleanup—great for when you're alone, a snap when you're having people over. If you're not sure what fish is seasonal, fresh, and delicious, ask the fish guy at your local supermarket. He'll tell you what's up.

Ingredients

1 cup coarsely chopped
   ripe tomato
⅓ cup pitted whole
   black olives
1 large garlic clove, minced
1 tablespoon coarsely chopped
   parsley
2 tablespoons olive oil plus
   some for the packets
2 6-ounce fillets of firm
   white fish: flounder, orange
   roughy, cod, halibut, snapper,
   or tilapia all work well
Salt and pepper to taste

Equipment

Small mixing bowl
Aluminum foil
Baking sheet

1. Preheat the oven to 400° F.
2. In a small mixing bowl, combine the tomato, olives, garlic, parsley, and olive oil.

3. Drizzle 2 teaspoons olive oil on a 12-inch sheet of aluminum foil and place one fish fillet in the center. Lightly salt and pepper the fillet, then spoon half the tomato mixture on top. Bring up the sides of the foil and fold over at the top to form a little tent with a sealed edge. This will create a steaming envelope for the fish. Prepare the other fillet the same way.

4. Place the packets on a baking sheet and bake for 10 to 15 minutes, until the fish is flaky and no longer transluscent. Gently remove the fish from the packets with a spatula and arrange on plates, scooping up the tomato and olives, too.

CHAPTER NINE

TAKING SIDES

Side Dishes

Uncle Ben is not your uncle. This much you know. But what's your side dish IQ otherwise? Chicken, meat, and tofu step out in style accompanied by light fluffy grains; pasta perks up next to a bed of garlic spinach. The right side dish can add color to a plate, give your stir-fry something to cuddle up next to, and round out the nutrition content of macaroni and cheese. Try not to play favorites—all of our side dishes make a lovely backdrop for your main attraction.

STALKER SALAD

Asparagus Vinaigrette

Serves 4
Prep time: 15 minutes
Cooking time: 5 minutes
. . . .

Beware of serving these steamed asparagus stalks to guests you don't plan on inviting back . . . or get ready to file for some restraining orders. Serve chilled as a lovely lunch side, or warm as an accompaniment to No Dish Fish (page 110) and Come Hither Couscous (page 118).

Ingredients

1 pound asparagus
¼ cup finely minced
   red onion
¼ cup finely minced red
   or yellow bell pepper
3 tablespoons olive oil
1 tablespoon Dijon mustard
3 tablespoons white wine
   vinegar
Salt and pepper to taste

Equipment

Pot with steamer basket
Medium mixing bowl

1. Trim the ends of the asparagus and steam for 5 minutes until tender but not mushy.
2. In a medium mixing bowl, combine the rest of the ingredients and set aside.
3. When the asparagus are ready, lay them in a shallow dish and drape with the vinaigrette.

RICE CAPADES

Coconut-Ginger Rice

Serves 4
Prep time: 5 minutes
Cooking time: 20 minutes

Coconut milk and ginger add subtle and delicate flavors to this sultry side dish. Try alongside Mojito Pork (page 96) or Girl Meets Soy (page 98).

Ingredients

1 cup canned unsweetened
   coconut milk, well stirred
1 cup chicken or vegetable
   broth
1 cup long-grain white rice
2 teaspoons grated fresh ginger
1 tablespoon finely minced
   cilantro
Dash of salt

Equipment

2-quart saucepan with lid

1. In a 2-quart saucepan, bring the coconut milk, broth, and rice to a boil. Reduce the heat to low and cover pot.
2. Simmer, covered, for 15 to 20 minutes, until all the liquid has been absorbed and the rice is tender.
3. Add the ginger and cilantro, fluff with a fork, and cover the pot again. Let the rice stand for 5 minutes while the flavors come together.
4. Add salt to taste before serving.

GREEN PARTY

Garlic Greens

Serves 2
Prep time: 2 minutes
Cooking time: 5 minutes

Hey diddle diddle, let's take a trip to the farmer's market. You'll be jumping over the moon—and running away with the spoon—when you taste these hearty greens flavored with garlic and lemon. A great accompaniment to Lazy Girl's Lasagna (page 104) or Mix 'n' Match Meatloaf (page 102).

Ingredients

2 tablespoons olive oil
1 large garlic clove,
   minced
20 ounces spinach leaves,
   washed
1 lemon, cut into wedges
Salt and pepper to taste

Equipment

4-quart saucepan

Heat the olive oil in a 4-quart saucepan and sauté the garlic for 2 to 3 minutes over medium heat until lightly browned. Add the spinach and stir frequently. When the spinach is completely wilted, turn off the heat. Squeeze the lemon wedges over the spinach and add salt and pepper to taste. Serve immediately.

CABBAGE PATCH KID

Crunchy Asian Slaw

Serves 4 to 6
Prep time: 5 minutes
· ·

So easy, a kid could make it. Serve alongside Wings of Desire (page 106) or Wrapsody (page 72).

Ingredients

¼ cup soy sauce
2 tablespoons Asian sesame oil
1 tablespoon sugar
1 teaspoon crushed red
    pepper flakes, optional
¼ cup white wine vinegar
1 white cabbage, shredded,
    or 1 16-ounce package shredded
    cabbage slaw mixture
2 tablespoons toasted sesame seeds

In a large mixing bowl, combine the soy sauce, sesame oil, sugar, red pepper flakes, if using, and vinegar. Add the cabbage and toss well to coat with the dressing. Serve garnished with sesame seeds, which you can toast, if you like, on the stovetop in a small skillet.

COME HITHER COUSCOUS

Lemon-Scented Couscous

Serves 4

Prep time: 5 minutes

Cooking time: 10 minutes

Light, lovely, and laced with lemon, Come Hither Couscous is the perfect taste bud temptress. Goes great with No Dish Fish (page 110) or On the Barbie (page 108).

Ingredients

1½ cups water or any
  kind of canned broth
1 cup couscous
2 tablespoons olive oil
1 teaspoon salt
1 teaspoon pepper
1 teaspoon grated
  lemon zest
1 teaspoon garlic powder
2 tablespoons minced
  parsley

Equipment

2-quart saucepan with lid

1. In a 2-quart saucepan, bring the water or broth to a boil. Add the couscous, olive oil, salt, and pepper. Stir briefly, then turn off the heat, cover, and let the couscous stand for 5 minutes, until all the liquid has been absorbed.

2. Fluff the couscous with a fork and add the lemon zest, garlic powder, and parsley. Adjust seasoning to taste.

GET CRACKIN'

Cracked Wheat Salad

Serves 4
Prep time: 2 minutes
Cooking time: 15 to 20 minutes

Quit complaining about boring sides, and dish up a few servings of bulgur, aka cracked wheat. When you're saying pshaw to potatoes, or turning your nose up at plain white rice, try this nutty, earthy, and versatile alternative alongside Girl Meets Soy (page 98) and Cabbage Patch Kid (page 117).

Ingredients

2 tablespoons olive oil
1 cup bulgur
2 cups chicken or vegetable broth
⅓ cup golden raisins
¼ cup toasted pine nuts
Salt and pepper to taste

Equipment

2-quart saucepan with lid

1. Heat the olive oil in a 2-quart saucepan and add the bulgur. Sauté the bulgur for 1 minute over medium-high heat, stirring constantly. Add the broth and bring to a boil. Cover.
2. Reduce the heat and cook, covered, until the grains are fluffy and light and all the liquid has been absorbed, about 15 to 20 minutes.
3. Let cool, then add the raisins and pine nuts, and salt and pepper to taste. Serve at room temperature or chilled.

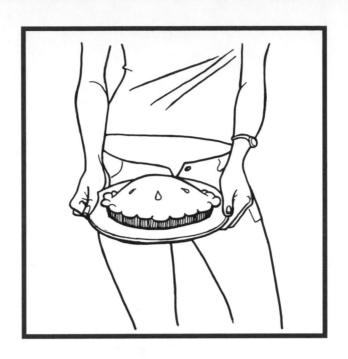

CHAPTER TEN

JUST DESSERTS

Sweets

Hey, sweetie pie. Get your mind out of the cookie jar. Packaged sweets and baked goods are chock-full of preservatives and strange added fats. Get back at the system by learning to make your own at home. Eating well is the best revenge, and our tart pies, rich brownies, and smart cookies are a clever way to get satisfaction. A fine meal requires a sweet finish, so come on—give yourself what you deserve.

BROWNIE DEAREST

Fudge Brownies

Makes 12 brownies
Prep time: 10 minutes
Baking time: 30 to 40 minutes

Joan Crawford may have freaked out over the smallest things, and that's not cool. But this delectable brownie is definitely something to get hysterical over. Served with fresh whipped cream and your favorite berries, everyone will be screaming for more. Just for the record, though, we think she was right about the wire hangers.

Ingredients

1 stick unsalted butter
½ cup all-purpose flour
½ cup unsweetened
   cocoa powder
1 cup sugar
1 teaspoon salt
2 large eggs, beaten
1 teaspoon vanilla extract

Equipment

9 by 9-inch baking dish
Large mixing bowl

1. Preheat the oven to 350° F. Grease a 9 by 9-inch baking dish and set aside.
2. Melt the butter in the microwave (will take about 45 seconds, but watch it to be sure).
3. In a large mixing bowl, combine the flour, cocoa powder, sugar, and salt.
4. Add the eggs, melted butter, and vanilla to the dry ingredients and continue to mix until well combined (as always, do not overmix).

5. Pour the batter into the baking dish and bake for 30 to 40 minutes, or until a knife inserted into the center comes out clean. Let the brownies sit for 10 minutes for easier cutting.

Playing the Field

Try adding these delicious extras:
- ¾ cup chopped maraschino cherries
- ¾ cup white chocolate chips
- ¾ cup toasted almonds
- 1 tablespoon grated orange zest

EVE'S APPLE

Tempting Apple Crisp

Serves 4 to 6
Prep time: 5 minutes
Baking time: 30 minutes

Poor Eve. So your guy thinks he knows everything—show him that you know a few things, too. Apples, cinnamon, and the easiest crumble ever make this quick dessert a snap, leaving plenty of time to get tossed out of Eden. Thirty minutes in the oven, and . . . paradise.

Ingredients

3 large apples, cored, peeled, and cut into 1-inch chunks
3 tablespoons sugar
1 tablespoon cinnamon
1 cup old-fashioned oats
3 tablespoons unsalted butter

Equipment

9 by 9-inch baking dish
Medium mixing bowl

1. Preheat the oven to 350° F.
2. Grease a 9 by 9-inch baking dish with butter. In a medium mixing bowl, combine the apples, 2 tablespoons of the sugar, and 2 teaspoons of the cinnamon. When the apples are well coated, transfer to the baking dish.
3. In the same mixing bowl, combine the oats, the remaining tablespoon of sugar and teaspoon of cinnamon, and the butter. Mix until butter is well integrated and the mixture develops a crumbly consistency.
4. Evenly distribute the oat mixture on top of the apples. Bake for 25 to 30 minutes, until slightly brown and crunchy on top. Goes great with You're Whipped! (page 126) or vanilla or caramel ice cream.

KEY-TO-MY-HEART LIME PIE

Cool and Creamy Key Lime Pie

Serves 6
Prep time: 15 minutes
Baking time: 15 minutes

Don't be a sourpuss. This Key-to-My-Heart Lime Pie has more return customers than a waitress in a Florida diner. Top it with You're Whipped! (page 126), and you'll get the keys to their cars, too.

Ingredients

4 egg yolks
One 14-ounce can
  sweetened condensed
  milk
½ cup lime juice (fresh squeezed
  is best, but bottled will do)
1 teaspoon grated lime zest
1 store-bought 8-inch graham
  cracker pie shell

Equipment

Large mixing bowl

1. Preheat the oven to 350° F.
2. In a large mixing bowl, beat the egg yolks and sweetened condensed milk together. When well combined, add the lime juice and zest, mixing everything together well.
3. Pour the filling into the pie shell and bake for 15 minutes. It will be slightly jiggly when you remove it from the oven but will set as it sits on the counter.
4. Refrigerate the pie when it cools to room temperature. Serve well chilled with You're Whipped! whipped cream.

YOU'RE WHIPPED!

Flavored Whipped Creams

Makes 2 cups
Prep time: 5 minutes
....

Yes, we know you like the spray cans of whipped cream, and that you aim them directly into your mouth when no one's looking. Well, maybe it's because you missed that day in home ec class when they showed you how easy it was to make real whipped cream from scratch.

Ingredients

1 cup cold heavy cream
3 tablespoons confectioners' sugar (powdered sugar)

Equipment

Medium mixing bowl
Hand mixer

1. Put a medium mixing bowl into the freezer for 5 minutes. (The colder the bowl, the quicker the cream will whip.)
2. Pour the cream into the cold bowl and beat with a hand mixer at moderate speed (increase the speed gradually so things don't splatter). After a few minutes it will start to look like, well . . . whipped cream. Add the sugar now (and any other flavors), a little bit at a time. Some people like it sweeter, so taste as you go.

Playing the Field

When it comes time to add the sugar, why not add flavor and flair as well?

- *Chocolate whipped cream:*
  Add 2 teaspoons unsweetened cocoa powder.
- *Cinnamon whipped cream:*
  Add 1 teaspoon cinnamon.

- *Vanilla whipped cream:*
  Add 2 teaspoons vanilla extract.
- *Mocha whipped cream:*
  Add 2 teaspoons powdered instant coffee
  and 1 teaspoon unsweetened cocoa powder
- *Lemon whipped cream:*
  Add ½ teaspoon grated lemon zest.
- *Whipped cream with a kick:*
  Add 1 tablespoon of your favorite rum or liqueur.

JUICY FRUIT

Fruit Salad with Honey-Lime Dressing

Serves 4

Prep time: 10 minutes

Dressing well isn't just for vegetables.

Ingredients

¼ cup fresh lime, lemon,
   or orange juice
¼ cup honey
1 teaspoon grated lemon,
   lime, or orange zest
1 tablespoon chopped mint,
   optional

1 cup cut-up cantaloupe,
   honeydew melon, or both
1 cup blueberries
1 cup sliced strawberries

Equipment

Large mixing bowl
Whisk

In a large mixing bowl, whisk together the juice, honey, zest, and mint, if using. Add the melon and berries, and toss with the dressing. Serve chilled.

SMART COOKIE
Multiple-Choice Cookie Recipe

Makes 2 dozen cookies
Prep time: 15 minutes
plus 1 hour fridge time
Baking time: 10 to 15 minutes

Smart Cookie makes it easy to win friends and influence people. This make-ahead, leave-in-the-fridge cookie dough is our answer to the stuff you love to buy at the grocery store and eat with a spoon. Roll, refrigerate, and bring it with you when you head for a friend's house. Ten minutes on a baking sheet, and no one will mind that you're about to win Trivial Pursuit, again.

Ingredients

4 tablespoons (½ stick)
   soft unsalted butter
¾ cup sugar
2 large eggs
2 teaspoons vanilla extract
½ cup all-purpose flour
2 teaspoons baking powder
½ teaspoon salt

Equipment

Large mixing bowl
Electric mixer
Plastic wrap
Baking sheet

1. In a large mixing bowl, combine the butter, sugar, eggs, and vanilla. Mix well.

2. Add the flour, baking powder, and salt. (If you're playing the field, here's where you add those extra ingredients.) Mix well. When the mixture forms a dough, divide it in two. Shape each half into a roll and wrap in plastic wrap. Refrigerate for at least 1 hour.

3. *To bake:* Preheat the oven to 350° F. Remove the plastic wrap and cut the dough into ¼-inch slices. Arrange the slices on a lightly greased baking sheet, leaving at least an inch or two between the slices. Bake for 10 to 15 minutes or until the edges are brown. Transfer the cookies right away to a rack or plate to cool completely; they will firm up as they cool.

Playing the Field

What makes a smart cookie smarter? Playing the field, of course . . .

Adding simple ingredients that you may have on hand is a great way to make a multitude of different cookies from one basic recipe.

- *Cinnamon Crunch Cookies:*
  Add 2 teaspoons cinnamon to the dough
  and sprinkle cookies with sugar before baking.
- *Cappuccino Chocolate Cookies:*
  Add 2 tablespoons finely chopped chocolate and
  1 tablespoon powdered instant coffee to the dough.
- *Lemon Tea Cookies:*
  Add 2 teaspoons grated lemon zest and
  2 tablespoons fresh lemon juice to the dough.
- *Pecan-Coconut Cookies:*
  Add ½ cup chopped pecans and ¼ cup shredded
  sweetened coconut to the dough.

ICE QUEEN

Elegant Ice-Cream Sandwiches

So, Your Royal Highness, are you too good for the lowly ice-cream sandwich? All those happy summer afternoons spent licking the ice cream out from between the chocolaty cookies, and now, nothing. We know it's because you're too busy and not because you're highfalutin . . . but still. You may be a lady, but you still need to feed your inner child. Now, stop fidgeting with that tiara and hook your loyal subjects up.

1. Get out your smart cookies, or grab a box of your favorite store-bought cookies.
2. Let a couple of pints of ice cream thaw until soft enough to spoon.
3. Lay the cookies bottoms-up on a tray lined with wax paper (make sure it'll fit in your freezer!). Put a couple of spoonfuls of ice cream on each cookie, then top with another cookie to make a sandwich. Put the tray in the freezer for a few minutes to let the sandwiches firm up, and enjoy!

Playing the Field

- Spread the cookies with peanut butter before adding the ice cream. Tastes great with chocolate chip cookies and chocolate or vanilla ice cream.
- Roll the ice-cream sandwiches in chopped nuts, sprinkles, or chopped chocolate chips for extra crunchy goodness.
- Try fun flavor combos: ginger snaps with green tea ice cream; lemon tea cookies with hazelnut ice cream; chocolate cookies with mint ice cream; pecan-coconut cookies with pistachio ice cream . . .

CHAPTER ELEVEN

SNACKS AND THE CITY

Menus

When fun beckons, a girl's got to grab her picnic basket and go. Send those overpriced pretzel pushers and street meat vendors packing and shimmy past the pimply teenager on deck at the movie concession stand with your stealthy snacks. Next time a flight attendant politely nudges you awake with the corner of a plastic tray bearing something that is meant to resemble a meal, remember, you're a pack-and-carry pro now, doll. You know where you want to go—and know you know what you'll be chewing on when you arrive. Instruction: Mix your grandmother with James Bond. Add a dash of Martha Stewart.

HANGOVER HELPER

Morning-After Menu

You had so much fun you can't remember how you got home last night; we just hope you recall inviting everyone to come over for breakfast. Brunch doctor says, take two aspirin and frittata in the morning.

Alotta Frittatas
(page 18): Add extra meat or cheese for more
headache-fighting goodness.
There's No Place Like Home Fries
(page 24)
Salad with Meanwhile, Back at the Ranch dressing
(page 41)
Bloody Murray cocktail
(page 89)—the hair of the dog . . .

LOVE BITES

Date Menu

You called, he answered. And now he's coming over for dinner. Woo him with:

Olive You tapenade
(page 71), served with soft white Italian bread
Salad with Colonel Mustard dressing
(page 42) and Get Your Crouton On
garlic croutons (page 45)
Mojito Pork stir-fry
(page 96) with Rice Capades ginger-coconut rice (page 115)
Love in a Time of Sangria cocktail
(page 88)
Key-to-My-Heart Lime Pie
(page 125) with You're Whipped! topping (page 126)

NAKED BRUNCH
The Brunch of Shame

Dinner went so well he stayed for breakfast. Start his day off right with our version of a very good morning.

French Toast Connection
> (page 16) made with last night's leftover Italian bread

Juicy Fruit salad
> (page 128)

Chai Me Up, Chai Me Down spiced tea
> (page 81)

THE BREAK-UP BAKERY
Love 'em and Leave 'em Menu

It was fun, but it's over. Break the news with our certified break-up bread.

Banana Split Bread
> (page 30)

Soda Jerk egg cream soda
> (page 78)

LUNCH LADY
Lunch at Home

Stop letting overpriced cafés bully you out of your lunch money— and treat yourself better than the cafeteria lady did.

Mango Lassie yogurt shake
> (page 79)

Wrapsody chicken wrap
> (page 72)

Cabbage Patch Kid slaw
> (page 117)

RUNNING LATE MENU

Midweek Dinner Party Menu

You've got seven people coming for dinner on Wednesday, and your boss just scheduled a late meeting. You'll be good to go with our Running Late Menu: get it ready the night before and pop it in the oven when you get home. A glass of red wine and a plateful of finger apps (baked yesterday) will distract your guests while you toss together:

Vermont, Italy, Vinaigrette

(page 44): Serve on a plate of mixed greens
alongside the lasagna.

Lazy Girl's Lasagna

(page 104): Build the night before and bake
when you get home.

Eve's Apple crisp

(page 124): Bake the night before and put it in
the oven for 5 minutes before serving to crisp up
the topping; serve à la mode.

Hot and Bothered spiked coffee

(page 91)

SNOW BUNNY

Blizzard Menu

You feel like you're in a little house in the big woods, with all the snow that's swirling around your abode. Get the cider going and make a pot of soup, because if you don't have a shovel, well, you're just going to have to wait until spring to leave your room. Good thing your beau came over to entertain you.

The Big Chili

(page 58)—warms you from the inside out

Mac and Jill macaroni and cheese
(page 64)
Green Party garlic greens
(page 116)
Along Came a Cider mulled apple cider
(page 83): Turn your kitchen into a haven.
Cinnamon Crunch Cookies
(page 129)

SULTRY SUPPER

Hot-Weather Menu

Designed for when it's hot and steamy and your flip-flops are lying under the table. You can't bear to have anything—even your cutie—too close, and the last thing you want to do is hang out near the oven. In fact, you'd like to climb into the fridge.

Why don't you, then? Dig around in there as if you have no idea what you're making. And then prepare:
Girlspacho chilled vegetable soup
(page 56)
Mixed greens with Memoirs of a Grapefruit dressing
(page 43)
Olive You tapenade
(page 71) on a baguette with fresh mozzarella
and tomato
Ice Queen ice-cream sandwiches
(page 132) with Lemon Tea Cookie (page 129)
and ginger ice cream

SAND WITCH

Beach Menu

Add some magic to a plain old beach day. Sunscreen, your favorite bikini, and a tote full of goodies stand in for eye of newt; a frozen bottle of water keeps you and your snacks from melting. Put a spell on 'em with:

Thermos of If Life Hands You Vodka cocktails
    (page 86)
Romeo and Jelly reinterpreted classic sandwiches
    (page 66)
Juicy Fruit salad
    (page 128)
Gingerbread Girl
    (page 32)

A TISKET, A TASKET

Picnic Menu

The second it's warm enough to sit outside with a light jacket, we head right over to one of our neighborhood parks. Music festivals make for a nice backdrop when they are in season; otherwise, watching hotties kicking a soccer ball around is plenty of entertainment. Remember to bring plates, cups, forks, and twice as many napkins as you think you'll need, and get your basket ready for some summer lovin' with:

Relish the Thought onion spread
    (page 69)
Curry Up! chicken salad
    (page 67)
Stalker Salad
    (page 114)
Pecan-Coconut Cookies
    (page 129)
Beer

SLUMBER PARTY

Girls' Night In Menu

Girls' night in, sleep not included. You've gathered the mamas, the movies, and the margarita glasses—now all you need are the munchies. Get the living room dance party going with:

Blenderella cocktail

    (page 87)

Shady Lady Pasta Puttanesca

    (page 100)

Ice Queen ice-cream sandwich bar

    (page 132)

TEST DRIVERS

· · · · · ·

The recipes in *Cheap & Easy* were all stirred and sautéed by the following people, who prepared breakfasts, lunches, dinners—and a round or two of cocktails—to make sure this book would run right. We lift our glasses to:

Vicki C. Abbinanti

Miriam Ackerman

Jenny Anmuth

Julietta Appleton

Kelly B. Archer

Nicole Diamond Austin

Julie Barer

Elana Benatar

Faye Bender

Molly Boren

Sarah Branham

Virginia Cepeda

Tatyana Charnis

Molly Chehak

Jenel Chesley

Carole Corrado

Katherine Darling

Rebecca Dhouni

Kelly Frank

Chris Franko

Cheryl Friedman

Keri Friedman

Claudia Gabel

Kate Garrick

Ashley Gold

Jody Handley

Megan Hickey

Amy Hirst

Alison Horn

Meghan Hubbard

Victoria Janis

JoAnn Kamuf

Jordan Kanfer

Lissy Katz

Karen Kosztolnyik

Katherine Kozack

Jessica Landy

Cindy Lee

Elizabeth Lesure

Penina and John Lopez

Marisa Moon

Laurie Motz

Stacy Notaras Murphy

Liz Nagle

Joanna O'Connell

Shannon O'Keefe

Devi Priya Pillai

Ruxandra Pond

Angela Rakis

Karin Rinderknecht

Emma K. Rothfeld

Claire H. Smith

Nikki Snyder

Lasca J. Sosseur

Charlotte Strick

Emily and Greg Takoudes

Anya Yurchyshyn

INDEX

• • • • • • •

ABOUT THE AUTHORS

· · · · · · ·

SANDRA BARK, a writer and cookbook editor, has been a vegetarian for more than ten years. ALEXIS KANFER has worked as a caterer, a chef, and a freelance food writer. Both women live in Brooklyn, NY, where they have small kitchens, tight budgets, and an appreciation for good food. Get in touch at www.cheapandeasycookbook.com